WEDDING
ETIQUETTE

WEDDING ETIQUETTE

Patricia and William Derraugh

Checklist by Gordon E. Porter

W. Foulsham & Co. Ltd.

London . New York . Toronto . Cape Town . Sydney

W. Foulsham & Company Limited
Yeovil Road, Slough, Berkshire, SL1 4JH
ISBN 0–572–01170–9

Copyright © 1983 W. Foulsham
& Co. Ltd.

Cover photograph courtesy of
Moss Bros. Ltd.

Photoset by
Rowland Phototypesetting Ltd,
Bury St Edmunds, Suffolk

Printed in Great Britain by
St Edmundsbury Press,
Bury St Edmunds, Suffolk

CONTENTS

Introduction	7
Getting Engaged	8
A Matter for the Law	13
England and Wales	13
Other Denominations	20
The Royal Navy	21
Scotland	22
Northern Ireland	24
Marriages Abroad	25
The Wedding Arrangements	26
The Time and Place	26
Invitations	27
The Wedding Presents	30
The Attendants	33
Dressing for the Occasion	35
The Flowers	37
The Photographs	38
The Press	39
Counting the Cost	39
The Bride's Special Day	42
The Marriage Ceremony	45
Church of England Weddings	45
Quaker Weddings	48
Roman Catholic Weddings	49
Jewish Weddings	50

The Reception 53
The Role of the Best Man 56
The Role of the Chief Bridesmaid 59
Toasts and Speeches 61
The Second Marriage 67
   A Divorce in the Family 68
Changing Your Name 70
The Honeymoon 72
Financing a Happy Marriage 74
Buying a House 79
Wedding Superstitions 86
Wedding Anniversaries 91
Personal Checklists 93
Index 126

INTRODUCTION

THERE ARE many ways of getting married and of celebrating the occasion, from the traditional "white wedding" and formal reception, to the register office ceremony with a buffet or party and "disco" afterwards. Making wedding arrangements also means thinking about flowers, invitations, wedding presents, a best man and bridesmaids and a whole host of other matters, as well as the ceremony itself. It can sometimes appear somewhat daunting, to say the least!

The chief aim of this book is to guide you through the legal, financial and family arrangements leading up to a marriage, and to help you enjoy a day which is, after all, intended to bring pleasure to all concerned. Whether you are bride or bridegroom, parent, best man or guest, you should find the answers to your questions in these pages.

But getting married does not, of course, stop with the wedding itself. For most people it brings personal and financial responsibilities that have not existed before, and later chapters look at these broader aspects of marriage, including finding and running a home and planning your own financial budget.

If, in the end, you can say that you have found the information you need for a successful wedding and a sure and practical start to married life, then the reasons for writing the book will have been justified – and the authors amply rewarded.

GETTING ENGAGED

MEN AND women will fall in love with each other as long as mankind exists. No-one can tell what it is that makes Patricia seem to Robert the most wonderful person on Earth and that life without her would be unbearable. Neither is there anything tangible that makes Patricia like Robert more than any other man she has met. The last people to be able to answer the question would be the couple themselves.

For many, falling in love marks the beginning of a new life, when everything seems brighter and more exciting and problems less burdensome as they are faced together.

However, by the same token, these first signs of love will not always lead to a lasting and satisfying relationship. The commitment to share your life with another person is a very real one and will bring about dramatic changes in your lifestyle. The time before the wedding gives you an opportunity to get to know each other better – a chance to think about your relationship and how you will "get on" – not as bride and bridegroom, but as husband and wife. If there are going to be any problems, it will be as well to know about them now.

Respect and affection for your partner will often prove just as important as the physical side of the relationship. One way of looking at this is to ask yourself: are you really good friends with your partner? Do you enjoy doing the same things and talking to each other? Do you respect what the other person has to say? It is not necessary to merge your identities but if there is not some measure of mutual respect and compatibility it could be a sign of difficulties ahead.

The question of finance is another area which is sometimes brushed aside in the belief that "we'll muddle through somehow". That may be, of course. There is nothing new or strange about married couples having to struggle a bit at first to make ends meet. But there may be problems if you cannot agree on priorities (a car, a home or a holiday, for example) or if one of you turns out to be an incurable spendthrift. If money is going to be tight, you should at least be sure that you can talk openly about how you are going to look after and manage it.

Important though they are, friends outside the marriage can also sometimes be rather a mixed blessing. How would you feel if your partner decided to go out with his or her friends without you? If the marriage means that you have to move a considerable distance from your old home, will you be able to adjust easily to a new set of friends? Are you both socially outgoing – or is one more inclined to stay at home?

None of these questions is particularly important in itself: there are no ideal conditions which have to be fulfilled before you get married. But what is important is that you should be able to discuss them openly and honestly with your partner and, if there are differences, that they can be accommodated in the relationship. The engagement gives you time to prepare for marriage, by making arrangements for the wedding, and also by thinking and talking about your future lives together.

Breaking the News

One of the first things to do when you get engaged is to tell both sets of parents. This is really a matter of courtesy. They will, after all, be concerned for your future well-being, anxious to meet the prospective son or daughter-in-law if they have not done so already, and will most likely be only too happy to become involved in helping you make plans and arrangements for the wedding.

Fortunately, the days of the grim "in laws" have largely disappeared. Very often a real affection grows up between the husband and his wife's parents or the wife and her husband's parents. It is also a good idea for the respective parents to meet and get to know each other as soon as possible. It will be a help to any marriage if there is good will all round between the members of the two families.

Near relatives also should be told of the engagement before the news is made public. If you intend to place a notice in the engagement columns of the local newspaper then close friends, too, would appreciate hearing the news in a more personal manner. This can be done formally by sending notices or letters to those concerned, or informally, over the telephone, or as an announcement at a party – or by a combination of all three.

Whichever method you choose, it is a good idea to make a list of everybody who is to be told and check it over with your parents beforehand. It is all too easy to inadvertently miss out the name of a relative or friend in the rush to let everyone know.

Letters, if you intend sending them, need not be lengthy, merely stating the name of your fiancé(e) and perhaps where you met and how long you have known each other. However, do try to send all the letters at the same time. That way no-one will feel hurt, even if they hear the news from another source before their own letter arrives.

The Rings

Engagement and wedding rings are traditionally thought of as the outward signs of your love and commitment to each other. The gemstone in the engagement ring and the unbroken circle of the wedding ring express the unique and permanent nature of your relationship. Not surprisingly, their significance and value to the wearer often increases over the years.

Choosing the rings is something you'll probably want to do together. There is a vast range to look at, so make a definite date to go round several jewellers and see if you can find ones which you both like.

Prices of rings vary enormously. You can spend almost as little or as much as you like. With wedding rings, refinements such as hand engraving can boost the cost considerably. On the other hand, old or antique rings can be very reasonable in price – and just as durable.

As a rule, an engagement ring is studded with stones, and the choice of these depends very much on personal preference. Often, the bride's lucky birth-stone is chosen, and diamonds of course are traditional favourites.

The following list gives the birth-stones and their meanings, with the months for which they stand.

January	Garnet, for Constancy.
February	Amethyst, for Sincerity.
March	Bloodstone, for Courage.
April	Diamond, for Innocence.
May	Emerald, for Success.

June	Pearl, for Health.
July	Ruby, for Love.
August	Sardonyx, for Married Happiness.
September	Sapphire, for Wisdom
October	Opal, for Hope.
November	Topaz, for Fidelity.
December	Turquoise, for Harmony.

Some couples decide to dispense with the engagement ring altogether and buy each other presents instead – usually something small and fairly permanent. But whether you opt for a ring, or presents, or if you would prefer just to go out for a celebration dinner, the choice is yours. After all, it's your engagement.

Breaking It Off

If, for some reason, you decide that you do not wish to proceed with the wedding, gifts received from relatives or friends as a result of the engagement should be returned. If you are still friends, you may decide to keep any presents given to each other during the engagement – or you can return those too.

If you have announced the engagement in the press, you should place a second announcement stating the marriage will no longer take place. It is usual for the girl to offer to return the ring, especially if she is the one to break off the engagement.

A MATTER FOR THE LAW

THERE ARE many ways, civil and religious, of taking the all-important step of getting married. This chapter deals with them mainly from the legal aspect.

ENGLAND AND WALES

In England and Wales a marriage can take place by means of (a) a civil ceremony (b) a ceremony performed in accordance with the rites of the Church of England or (c) a ceremony performed in accordance with the rites of any other religious denomination.

Church of England
A marriage in accordance with the rites of the Church of England may be contracted in one of four ways:

(i) By publication of banns.
(ii) By common licence (ordinary licence).
(iii) By special licence.
(iv) On the authority of a licence issued by a superintendent registrar.

Generally, both parties to the marriage will be expected to be members of the Church of England and at least one of them should live in the parish of the church where the marriage is to take place (although certain exceptions as to residence may be made – for example in the case of marriage by special licence or sometimes if a person is an established member of a church outside his or her home parish and has his or her name entered on the electoral roll of that parish).

(i) Publication of Banns This is the method traditionally preferred by most people. The first thing to do is to call upon the minister of the church in which the marriage is to be solemnized and to ask him to allow the ceremony to take place in his church. If you would like another minister to officiate at the wedding (an old friend of the family, for example) that should also be discussed. When all the preliminaries have been satisfactorily completed, the minister will proceed to publish the banns.

The banns are published by being read aloud in church on three successive Sundays preceding the ceremony. They are usually read at the main service of the church. It is usual for the couple to be in church on at least one of the three occasions when the banns are read.

When the couple do not live in the same parish, the banns must be read in duplicate (a) in the parish of the man and (b) in the parish of the woman. A certificate should be obtained from the minister whose church is not being used to give to the minister in whose church the ceremony is to take place. This certificate states that the banns have been legally called, and without it the officiating minister cannot proceed with the wedding service.

Once the banns have been published, the wedding may be solemnized on any day within the three following months. It is best not to leave it too late. Marriages sometimes have to be delayed, and if there is insufficient time to arrange an alternative date within the three months the banns will have to be called again.

Since the system of marriage by banns has been devised to give publicity to the forthcoming wedding, it is fraudulent to substitute misleading names for the proper ones. When a person is generally known by a name which is not the one shown on his or her birth certificate, the banns should give the name more generally known, or should include both.

(ii) Common Licence (Ordinary Licence)   The advantages of being married by common licence are that banns are unnecessary and only one clear day's notice is needed before the licence to marry is issued. It is therefore a much quicker procedure, and especially useful when for some reason the banns have not been properly published.

Common licences may be obtained from the Faculty Office, 1 The Sanctuary, Westminster, London S.W.1., or from the Bishop's Register Office (situated in every cathedral town) or from one of the Surrogates for granting licences in the diocese – the minister at the church where the wedding is to take place may hold this title; if he does not, he will be able to tell you where you can obtain the licence.

In applying at any of the above offices, it is necessary that one of the parties to the marriage should appear in person. The person making the application is required to sign a declaration stating that there is no legal reason why the marriage cannot properly take place and that either the man or the woman, or both, have lived for at least fifteen days prior to the application within the area served by the church that is to be used for the ceremony.

(iii) Special Licence   Special licences are issued only by the Archbishop of Canterbury at the Faculty Office, 1 The Sanctuary, Westminster, London S.W.1., and in cases when there is some special and urgent reason why the more ordinary methods of solemnizing the marriage are unsuitable. When granted, a special licence permits the wedding to take place at any time (within three months of the date of issue) and in any place, without restriction as to the residence of either party.

(iv) Superintendent Registrar's Certificate   A certificate to marry in accordance with the rites of the Church of England may also be given by a Superintendent Registrar.

The church where the marriage is to take place must be situated within the registration district of the Superintendent Registrar and either the man or the woman must have lived in the parish for seven days prior to giving notice.

The certificate will not be issued until twenty-one days after the notice is entered in the notice book and the ceremony may then take place within three months *from the day on which the notice was entered*. The marriage may be solemnized only by a minister of the Church of England and with the consent of the minister whose church is being used for the ceremony.

This method of authorisation is, however, very rarely used.

Before a Registrar
When, for whatever reason, the couple do not wish to marry in a church, the ceremony can take place under civil law in a register office. In England and Wales notice

should be given to the local Superintendent Registrar (whose address can be found under "Registration of Births, Deaths and Marriages" in the telephone directory) who will arrange the marriage in one of three ways:

(i) By Superintendent Registrar's Certificate.
(ii) By Superintendent Registrar's Certificate and Licence.
(iii) By Registrar General's Licence.

With the exception of a licence issued by the Registrar General, notice may also be personally "attested" before any local registrar of births and deaths or local registrar of marriages, but the notice is not held to have been duly given until it is received by the Superintendent Registrar and entered in his book.

(i) Superintendent Registrar's Certificate   The official in this case will complete a form giving the names of the parties wishing to be married, their residences and their ages. The form also requires mention of the building in which the marriage is to take place and concludes with a declaration, to be signed, which states that there is no legal objection to the marriage.

Both the man and the woman must have lived in the area controlled by the registrar for seven days prior to giving notice, in which case only one of them need appear to make the declaration: or, if they live in different registration districts, they must each make the declaration before their own registrar and they must each have lived in their respective areas for seven days prior to the visit.

On being satisfied with the information supplied to him, the Superintendent Registrar will make the necessary entry in his notice book and, twenty-one days later, he will issue the certificate for the marriage. The ceremony can then take place at any time within the three months *following the entry in the notice book.*

(ii) Superintendent Registrar's Certificate and Licence For marriage by certificate and licence, a similar declaration must be made and signed as for a marriage by certificate, but the residential qualifications are different. Only one of the couple need give notice, even though they may live in different registration areas, provided that one of them has lived in the area for fifteen days prior to the visit. However, the person not appearing must be within the borders of England and Wales or have his or her usual place of residence in England or Wales at the time notice is given.

One clear day after entering the notice, the Superintendent Registrar will issue the licence for the marriage (Sunday, Christmas Day and Good Friday are not counted). The licence is valid for three months following the date of entry in the notice book.

(iii) Registrar General's Licence This method was introduced in 1970 and is reserved for cases of extreme illness where it would be impossible for the marriage to take place in a register office or other registered building. The licence permits the marriage to be solemnized in any place and at any time within three months from the date of entry in the notice book. There is no residence qualification and no statutory waiting period before the licence is issued. Notice of marriage must be given (in person) by one of the couple to the local Superintendent Registrar.

Keeping on the Right Side of the Law
In addition to the formal procedures which have to be observed before any marriage can take place, there are a

number of essential regulations concerning the conduct of the wedding ceremony itself and the freedom (in law) of the parties to marry.

(i)   With the exception of the Jewish and Quaker ceremonies, the special licence and a licence issued by the Registrar General, no wedding can take place before 8.00 am or after 6.00 pm.

(ii)   A wedding cannot be private – hence the doors are not to be locked while the ceremony is proceeding.

(iii)   Before the ceremony, all relevant certificates or licences must be produced and handed to the registering official.

(iv)   Two persons must be present at the wedding, who will be required to sign their names as witnesses to the ceremony. They can be total strangers to each other and to the couple about to be married.

(v)   People under 16 years of age may not marry. In the case of a person over 16 but under 18 consent to marry must be given by the parents or other lawful guardians or guardian.

(vi)   The marriage will not be valid if either party is already married.

(vii)   Neither party to a divorce may re-marry until the "decree absolute" has been granted.

(viii)   The parties must be respectively male and female by birth.

(ix)   Both parties must be acting by consent and be of sufficiently sound mind to understand the nature of a marriage contract.

(x)   Marriages are forbidden between people who are closely related. Those relationships prohibited *by law* are listed below. Additional restrictions may apply when a marriage is to be performed according to the rites of some religious denominations.

Prohibited Degrees of Relationship   You may not marry your: mother, adoptive mother, former adoptive mother, father, adoptive or former adoptive father, daughter, adoptive daughter, former adoptive daughter, son, adoptive or former adoptive son, father's mother, father's father, mother's mother, mother's father, son's daughter, son's son, daughter's daughter, daughter's son, sister, brother, wife's mother, husband's father, wife's daughter, husband's son, father's wife, mother's husband, son's wife, daughter's husband, father's father's wife, father's mother's husband, mother's father's wife, mother's mother's husband, wife's father's mother, husband's father's father, wife's mother's mother, husband's mother's father, wife's son's daughter, husband's son's son, wife's daughter's daughter, husband's daughter's son, son's son's wife, son's daughter's husband, daughter's son's wife, daughter's daughter's husband, father's sister, father's brother, mother's sister, mother's brother, brother's daughter, brother's son, sister's daughter, sister's son.

OTHER DENOMINATIONS

If the marriage is to be conducted according to the rites of a religious denomination other than the Church of England, notice of marriage must still be given to the authorised registrar for the area concerned, who will grant a licence.

The chapel or building where the marriage is to take place must normally be registered for marriages, and the registrar or other authorised person (usually the minister) must be present to register the marriage.

At some point in the ceremony, as with any wedding, each of the contracting parties (the persons getting married) must make the following declaration:

"I do solemnly declare that I know not of any lawful impediment why I (full name) may not be joined in matrimony to (full name)."

Then each must say:

"I call upon these persons here present to witness that I (full name) do take thee (full name) to be my lawful wedded wife/husband."

THE ROYAL NAVY

If one of the parties to the marriage is a serving member of the Royal Navy, the banns may be published aboard ship by the chaplain or commanding officer. In the case of a wedding in a register office or other registered building the commanding officer may record the particulars in place of the registrar and issue the necessary certificate twenty-one days after notice has been given.

SCOTLAND

In times past, many a runaway couple was married at Gretna Green, when they would have been forbidden to wed under the more restrictive English law. Today, Scottish law does not allow "irregular" marriages – such as by declaration before two witnesses – but the rules are still not the same as in England, Wales or Northern Ireland.

The law on marriage in Scotland is now governed by The Marriage (Scotland) Act 1977. You can be married by a registrar, or assistant registrar, and the wedding will normally be held in his office. Alternatively, if you want a religious ceremony, you can be married by any clergyman, parson, priest or officer of any denomination who is entitled to undertake marriages under the Marriage (Scotland) Act. Whatever type of wedding you have, there must be two witnesses present who are at least 16 years of age.

In order to set the wedding wheels in motion, the couple must each get a marriage notice form from a registrar of births, marriages and deaths in Scotland. It does not matter which registrar is initially approached, but when the forms are filled in, they must be returned to the registrar for the district where the ceremony is to take place. Ideally this should be done a month or more before the wedding date, and except in very exceptional circumstances a minimum of fifteen days notice must be given. If either party has been married before, the notice period is six weeks.

The marriage notice form is designed to establish whether you are eligible to get married – for example in terms of your age, existing marital status and sex – and that you are not related to your intended spouse in any way which forbids marriage. You have to sign a declaration that the information you give is true; if it is not, your marriage will not be valid.

When you return your marriage notice form, you will also have to give the registrar your birth certificate. If either party has been married before, you will also have to produce a death certificate of your former spouse, or a copy of the divorce decree, remembering that a decree nisi from a court outside Scotland is not sufficient. If either party is domiciled outside the United Kingdom, you will have to show that there is no legal reason in your own country why you should not be married. When producing any foreign documents, it is important to get a certified translation, and if there is any doubt about what is needed, you should ask the registrar.

If there is a delay in getting any of the documents you need, it is best to return your marriage notice form anyway, explain the situation, and get the documents to the registrar as soon as you can.

The registrar will check the facts given on the marriage notice form and then prepare a marriage schedule. For a civil marriage he will keep the schedule in his office until the wedding; but if you are having a religious ceremony, one of you must collect it, in person, not more than a week before the wedding. After the ceremony you must both sign the schedule, as must your two witnesses and whoever conducted the wedding. The schedule must be returned to the registrar within three days so that he can register the marriage.

As well as getting the marriage notice organised in good time, it is important to inform the person who will perform the ceremony of the date on which you want to be married. Particularly in towns, and at popular times of year, you may need to book early.

If you live in England or Wales but are marrying someone who lives in Scotland (or whose parents live in Scotland) and want your wedding to be in Scotland, it is possible to give notice without actually going north of the border to do so. Notice must be given to the Superintendent Registrar where you live, and your partner must give notice in Scotland in the normal way. Notices issued in England and Wales are valid in Scotland and vice-versa, provided only one of the parties is resident in Scotland. However, marriage by licence in a register office in England or Wales is not possible in this case.

NORTHERN IRELAND

In Northern Ireland, notice to marry is given to the District Registrar of Marriages, the residence qualification is seven days. Marriage can take place by licence, special licence, banns, certificate from a registrar or licence from a District Registrar of Marriages.

Notices issued in Northern Ireland are valid in England and Wales and vice-versa, but, as in Scotland, marriage by licence in a register office in England or Wales is not possible when one of the parties is resident in Northern Ireland.

MARRIAGES ABROAD

If you intend to marry abroad you should first find out what documents (if any) will be required for the marriage to be legal. You will probably be asked to provide a certificate of no impediment to marriage and you may also need your birth certificate, proof of residence, proof of no convictions, etc. The extent of the requirements varies according to the regulations of each country. If you are still living in Britain, you should check with the foreign consul of the country concerned.

The marriage will generally be held to be legally valid under British law provided that it is performed in accordance with the law of the country in which it takes place and that none of the regulations in British law regarding the relationship of the parties or their freedom to marry are contravened. The marriage must also be monogamous. However, the situation varies according to individual circumstances and final judgement may rest on a court decision.

WITH THESE DOCUMENTS
I THEE WED

THE WEDDING ARRANGEMENTS

T HE ANNOUNCEMENT of your engagement is the first step in the process of getting married and marks the beginning of much careful planning and preparation for the wedding day itself.

THE TIME AND PLACE

Once you have decided on the form of ceremony you would like and roughly when it is to take place you should go to see the minister or registrar concerned so that the proper religious and/or legal arrangements can be made.

If you are going to be married in church, you should discuss with the minister the details of the ceremony including the style and order of service, whether or not a choir should be present, the music that is to be played and the possibility of bell ringing. Also find out about the fees (there are basic legal statutory fees but other church costs are at the discretion of the minister) and ask if your guests will be allowed to take pictures in the church or throw confetti in the church grounds. Probably several meetings will be needed. The minister will want to talk to you about the significance of a church wedding, and he may invite you to attend a marriage preparation course which takes a broad look at all the issues involved.

In all aspects of the marriage ceremony the minister really is the expert and his advice and guidance will be well worth having.

Equally, if you have decided on a civil ceremony, you should go to see the local Superintendent Registrar as soon as possible. Apart from the legal formalities, you should find out how many guests can be accommodated at the ceremony and whether photographs may be taken in the register office.

Most people deciding to get married in this way do so either because they want a quiet ceremony with no fuss or because a marriage in church would conflict with their own beliefs.

Some people, however, think that because one or other of them is divorced, they have no option but to get married in a register office. This is not the case. Although the marriage cannot usually take place in an Anglican church, often another church can be found where the minister will be prepared to conduct the ceremony. The Superintendent Registrar may advise you on this if you are not sure who to approach.

As an alternative, you could have a civil wedding followed by a Service of Blessing in church. The bride and bridegroom, together with friends and relations, meet in the church: the minister gives a brief address and there are prayers to bless the marriage.

INVITATIONS

The invitations should be sent out well in advance of the date set for the wedding – six to eight weeks is about right.

The list of guests is usually drawn up by the bride and her mother in consultation with the bridegroom and his parents. The engagement list will serve as a useful guide, although there are sure to be some omissions and additions.

The invitations themselves are normally composed in the third person and sent from the bride's parents. The most popular wording is:

Mr & Mrs Edgar Smith
request the pleasure of
the company of

....
(write the name of the guest(s))
at the marriage of their daughter
Patricia
to
Mr Robert Brown
at All Saints Church
Kingsgrove
on Saturday 27 April
at 2-45 pm
and afterwards at a reception at
The Bell Inn, Kingsgrove

RSVP
21 Firhill Lane,
Kingsgrove,
Kent

An alternative version could read:

> *Mr & Mrs Edgar Smith*
> *request the pleasure of your company*
> *at the marriage of their daughter*
> *Patricia*
> *to Mr Robert Brown*
> *etc.*

In this case the name(s) of the guest(s) are written on the top left hand corner of the card.

The exact wording depends on who is issuing the invitation and their relationship to the bride. For example, if the bride's mother is a widow or her parents are divorced and her mother has remarried the invitation could read:

> *(Mr &) Mrs Robert Jones*
> *request(s) the pleasure of*
> *the company of*
>
> *....................*
>
> *at the marriage of her*
> *daughter*
> *Patricia (Smith)*
> *etc.*

Although the bride's surname is rarely included in the wording it can be appropriate in cases where it differs from that of the host and hostess.

If the number of guests is quite low, the invitations may be written by hand on suitably attractive stationery. More often, however, they are printed. Visit a stationers and have a look at the range of cards and styles of lettering that are available. Black is the traditional colour for the lettering. If you want to order reply cards, Order of Service sheets or cake boxes, you can see to this at the same time.

In the unfortunate event of a family bereavement or severe illness you will probably want to postpone the wedding, and notices will have to be sent to all those invited to attend. A plain statement of the facts is quite sufficient, with notice of the new date for the wedding, if one has been arranged:

> *Owing to the recent death (illness) of Mr Edgar Smith, the wedding between Patricia Smith and Mr Robert Brown at All Saints Church, Kingsgrove at 2.45 pm on Saturday 27 April has been postponed (to 4.00 pm on Friday 30 May).*

Formal replies to invitations should be sent promptly (within three days of receiving the invitation) and are also traditionally drawn up in the third person. The following is the usual wording:

> *Mr and Mrs John Clemence thank Mr and Mrs Edgar Smith for their kind invitation to their daughter's wedding and to the reception and will be most happy to attend.*

However, when the guests are very close friends of the host and hostess a brief, informal thank-you note will do just as well.

THE WEDDING PRESENTS

The business of giving or receiving wedding presents is always a little daunting – to both sides. Visions of dozens of toasters and electric kettles loom before the eyes of the engaged couple, while the guests are naturally concerned that their carefully chosen gifts should be received with the proper appreciation.

Even the best laid plans go wrong sometimes – but there are some practical steps you can take to ensure that this particular wedding custom turns out happily (as far as possible) for all concerned.

There are really only two rules to remember:

(i) Have a wedding present list prepared for anyone who wishes to consult it.

(ii) Be sure to write thank-you letters to everyone who sends you a present.

(i) The Wedding List

One way of organising the wedding list is to approach a department store which offers a special wedding gift service. The bride and bridegroom visit the store and make a note of all the items they would like to receive as presents. The store then draws up a comprehensive list which the guests then refer to when they are deciding what to buy.

If the store does not offer a mail order service, and it is inconvenient for some guests to shop there, they can be sent a copy of the latest version of the list. As soon as a present is received, the bride informs the store and the list is amended. Alternatively, a different, smaller wedding list is sent, in which case the guests each choose a present, cross it off the list and return it to the bride.

If you would rather not go to a department store, simply extend this method to include all the guests. There will still be a risk of duplication, but not nearly as much as if you leave your guests without any suggestions at all, and in practice, most people will check with you first before going ahead with their chosen purchase.

The list itself should contain a good number of inexpensive as well as expensive presents, and should run to more items than you actually expect to receive. This avoids the possibility of the last guest to see the list being left to buy the colour television set!

Traditional wedding presents include items of china, glass, cutlery and kitchen utensils, garden tools, linens and other home accessories. More expensive gifts such as carpets and furniture are usually reserved for very close relatives or groups of friends banding together to share the costs.

There is, however, no reason why you should think only in terms of fitting out the home. Books, pocket calculators, typewriters or sports equipment may be more useful to you and more urgently required. So do consider what your real needs are before finally drawing up the list.

(ii) Thank-you Letters

Although you can, if you like, ignore the need for a wedding list and perhaps even survive the resultant chaos, the same cannot be said of rule (ii) – the need to write thank-you letters. It is so obviously discourteous and hurtful not to thank people who sent you presents that you should be especially careful not to leave anybody out.

A methodical approach is the only answer. Whenever you receive a present, make a note of what it is, who sent it and when it arrived. Write to the person concerned as soon as possible, thanking them for the gift and put a tick against their name when the letter is in the post.

This task traditionally falls to the bride, but if the bridegroom has received any personal gifts, he should reply to the senders on his own behalf.

Displaying the Presents

It is natural for the guests to want to see the wedding presents, and a display may be arranged at the reception or in the bride's parents' home. But there are certain risks involved. If the display is to be at an outside reception, perhaps at a big hotel, there may be a chance of some petty thieving from uninvited "guests". Moreover you will be effectively advertising the contents of your future home to anyone who happens to be in the vicinity.

For that reason it is usually safer to stage the display at a private house. The only snag is that some guests may feel embarrassed to see their own relatively inexpensive presents ranged against other more valuable items. It will help if you dispense with the usual custom of using name tags to accompany the presents: if cheques have been received, you could set out cards stating simply "cheque from . . .' without divulging the amounts. The same applies to a display set up at the reception.

THE ATTENDANTS

The best man should be chosen very early on in the proceedings and ideally, should be someone with an ability to organise and get things done with humour and tact – besides being a long-standing friend of the bridegroom.

The reality, of course, may be very different; the chosen friend may well be terrified at what lies ahead. However, most people manage very well once they find out what is expected of them and set about making the arrangements for the wedding day.

Together, the bridegroom and the best man choose the ushers (if there are to be any) whose main role will be to show the wedding guests to their seats in the church, hand out service sheets or hymn books and make sure that everyone has transport to the reception – and knows how to get there! They also escort the bridesmaids from the church so, typically, there will be the same numbers of ushers as bridesmaids.

The chief bridesmaid is most often either a very close friend or sister of the bride. Although not so concerned as the best man with making arrangements for the wedding, she will have plenty to do in assisting the bride, often helping to choose the dresses and flowers, as well as offering a good deal of personal support.

Most brides choose three bridesmaids but there's nothing to stop you having none at all, or just one, or as many as eight. It's really up to you. It is customary for the bride and bridegroom to give each of them a present in recognition of their services – often a small piece of jewellery which can be worn at the ceremony. A gift for the best man is usual, too.

Small children may also sometimes play a part in the bridal procession. Very young children can be very appealing, but there is always a chance that they may decide at the last moment to play the unconscious role of the *enfant terrible*. If married, the chief bridesmaid, is known as a matron of honour.

DRESSING FOR THE OCCASION

Choosing a wedding dress that will look and feel absolutely right on the day is one of the most important (and enjoyable) decisions the bride must make during the run-up to the ceremony.

The eventual choice will largely depend on the significance you attach to the dress itself and the sort of wedding you would like it to be. You may opt for the traditional white silk or lace dress with head-dress and veil, or choose a different colour such as cream or oyster, or a patterned dress.

If the wedding is to take place in a register office, you can still wear a traditional "white wedding" dress, if that is what you would really like.

Whichever kind of dress you choose, give yourself plenty of time to look around and try on different examples. You should also allow time for the dress to be altered, if necessary, or made, if you are having one specially designed or made from a pattern.

Dresses for the Bridesmaids

The bride chooses the bridesmaids' dresses, the main criteria being that they should complement her own wedding outfit. A dramatic contrast in colour, for example, will do little to enhance the bridal procession – or the wedding photographs. It might also look a little odd if the bride appeared in a plain dress while the bridesmaids were adorned with frills and lace. Bear in mind, too, that bridesmaids vary in size, shape and colouring. You are trying to find something to suit them all, so avoid too much finery, or colours that are too strident.

Male Fashion

If the wedding is to be a very formal affair, the principal men will wear morning suits. This includes the bridegroom, the best man, the ushers and both fathers.

Generally, morning suits are either all grey or consist of a black tailed coat and pin striped trousers. They look good in the wedding photographs with accessories such as hats and gloves, although these can be rather a nuisance as more time will be spent carrying them and getting them mixed up than actually wearing them.

Shoes and socks, shirts and ties (never black) should be chosen to match each other. A black suit might call for a white shirt, grey or cream tie and black shoes. With a grey suit, a white or blue shirt, blue or grey tie and black shoes will tone in well.

The morning suits may be hired or bought off the peg, or you could have one tailor made. They are expensive to buy, but will often last a long time so if you are likely to attend many other formal events where a morning suit is required you could take the opportunity to buy one now. For the majority, however, hiring a suit will be the best answer. Remember that the summer months are the most popular for weddings and formal social functions and reserve your suit well in advance.

The alternative for some weddings is a well-cut two- or three-piece lounge suit – which will form a welcome addition to your wardrobe after the great event. Cream or white suits can look very effective, and velvet jackets in black or rustic colours worn with plain or dress shirts are also very fashionable. The principal men should, however, take their cue from the bridegroom when deciding what to wear. They should not outshine him on the big day.

THE FLOWERS

Flowers are a very important part of every church wedding. Usually there will be bouquets or posies for the bride and bridesmaids and buttonholes for the principal men, and the church and reception area will be decorated with displays. There may also be sprays or corsages for the two mothers, and the bride may wish to wear a head-dress of fresh flowers or attach just one flower to her hair or veil.

You will be able to choose the bouquets from a selection of designs when you see the florist – who will also be the best person to ask about suitable flowers for the church and reception.

If the arranging is not to be carried out professionally, the flowers may still need to be ordered several weeks in advance of the ceremony, especially if you want unusual or out of season flowers. They should not be collected until one or two days before the wedding, when the larger displays are arranged. The bouquet, buttonholes and other dress flowers are usually delivered or collected on the morning of the wedding and the dress flowers are distributed at the church before the ceremony.

You will need to get the permission of the minister to decorate the church, and arrange a time when this can be conveniently carried out. He may be able to suggest someone who can help you in return for a small donation.

You could also combine with other couples who are getting married in the church on the same day – the minister should be able to supply names and addresses.

When you are choosing the flowers, remember to take into account the character and size of the church and reception areas. A large, formal display, for example, would look out of place in a small room or a country church. It is also a good idea to have a theme – of colours and/or varieties – running through from the bride's bouquet to the flowers used in the church and reception. As with the wedding dresses, aim for a sympathetic blend of colour and form.

If the wedding is to take place in a register office, it may already be decorated with flowers. Check with the Superintendant Registrar. If not, you may be able to arrange for a simple display to be set up before the ceremony.

THE PHOTOGRAPHS

You will probably have plenty of offers from friends and relations to take photographs at the wedding: however, if you want good-quality pictures which cover all or most aspects of the wedding it is best to play safe and hire the services of a professional photographer.

Prices – and the sort of package you will be offered – vary considerably. Don't automatically accept the cheapest quote, unless you are only really bothered that the pictures should "turn out". Go on recommendations, and ask to see examples of the photographer's work. Styles differ, and the photographer whose overall treatment you admire most is probably the one for you.

Pictures may be taken of all the major events, usually beginning at the bride's home before she leaves for the church and ending with the couple's departure on honeymoon. You should check with the minister to see if photographs will be allowed at the ceremony itself.

When you're ordering prints from the photographer,

think about ordering two additional sets for each of your parents. They make great "thank you" presents – if you can afford them.

As well as the traditional album of wedding photographs, there are plenty of audio-visual firms who will offer to film the wedding and put it on videotape. Costs and coverage are comparable to photographs, and extra cassettes are relatively inexpensive.

THE PRESS

Even if the engagement has not been announced in a newspaper, many couples like to insert a notice giving the time and place of the forthcoming wedding, to appear a few days before the chosen date. Newspapers usually have their own style for this, so check in the one you want to use for a suitable wording.

The newspaper may also publish an account of the wedding, sometimes by sending a reporter/photographer, but more often by issuing a standard form to be filled in and returned after the wedding with a photograph.

COUNTING THE COSTS

Even a small, quiet wedding will have fees and expenses to be met, and although the traditional rules of payment no longer strictly apply, it is as well to know who is normally expected to pay for what – even if only to thank others when they offer to share the costs.

Traditionally, the bride's father finds himself financially crippled. He is supposed to pay for:

(i)   Announcements, invitations and photographs.
(ii) Bride's dresses.
(iii) Flowers to decorate the church and reception.
(iv) Transport to the church for himself, the bride, the bride's mother and bridesmaids; to the reception for himself and the bride's mother.
(v) The reception.

The reception is usually the biggest expense and the bridegroom's father and the bridegroom himself will often share the costs. The bride and bridegroom may pay for the press announcements and help with the cost of the wedding invitations and photographs. Normally, the bride pays for the wedding dress. Traditionally the bridesmaids paid for their own dresses, however this does imply an obligation for the bride to choose a style which would be suitable for some subsequent occasion. Today, in practice, most parties decide according to their own circumstances, but if the dresses are not likely to be worn again, then the bride should offer to meet the expense.

Traditional costs for the bridegroom are somewhat less. He pays for:

(i)   The engagement and wedding rings.
(ii) All legal and church costs (licence, choir, etc.).
(iii) Bouquets and dress flowers for the bride and bridesmaids, the two mothers and the principal men.
(iv) Presents for the bridesmaids, the best man and the ushers.
(v) The stag party.
(vi) Transport to the church for himself and the best

man; and to the reception for himself and the
bride.

(vii) The honeymoon.

With the exception of the stag party, at which no more
than a round of drinks may be called for, the bridegroom
should expect to settle all these costs – with the help of the
bride where appropriate.

If the bridegroom is to have a wedding ring, the bride
should pay for that, and she may also like to buy presents
to give to her mother and father on the day of the wedding.

YOUR ROUND GROOM

THE BRIDE'S SPECIAL DAY

E VERY BRIDE wants to look her best on her wedding day, when she will be the centre of attention for the bridegroom and all the guests, and the feature of the wedding photographs.

Remember, you don't have to be a beauty queen in order to play the role of the radiant bride; your own happiness and sense of exhilaration will already show in your appearance and expression. However you can make the most of this natural radiance by some careful preparation in the weeks before the wedding.

Beauty comes from within – and that means a healthy diet – lots of fresh fruit, vegetables and salads – coupled with exercise, to keep your skin well toned and your figure trim. Good grooming is important too; nails should be manicured and your hair could be professionally cut and conditioned to give it extra body and shine. Choose a style that complements your head-dress if you have one. It's best not to experiment too much with your make-up – and certainly not on the morning of the wedding. You probably know what suits you best, so stick to what you're familiar with and allow extra time to apply it to your own satisfaction. Your mother can carry a make-up bag so that you can freshen up when you arrive at the reception.

The big events of the day really begin when the photographer arrives at to take pictures at your parents' house before the ceremony. As well as photographs with your mother and father, it's a good idea to have some taken of the final stages of putting on the wedding dress.

Before the bridesmaids leave for the church you could present them with their gifts, especially if you have chosen jewellery which can be worn at the ceremony. If you have a present for your mother and father, you could give this to them now or leave it for them to find after the wedding.

At the church entrance, the chief bridesmaid will meet you and make sure that the dress and veil are properly arranged. You take your father's right arm to walk up the aisle to where the bridegroom and best man are waiting. The chief bridesmaid will take the bouquet to leave your hands free when the ring is put on. Following the marriage service, you accompany the bridegroom into the vestry to sign the register – which you do first, in your maiden name. Bride and bridegroom then lead the procession out of the church, with the bride taking the left arm of her husband.

When the photographs have been taken, you will be the first to leave for the reception, where you will form part of the receiving line to (briefly) welcome the guests.

The bride does not have to make a speech at the reception, but if you do want to say some personal words of thanks, the best time is just after the bridegroom has responded to the main toast. It would then be usual for the bridegroom to rise again to propose the toast to the bridesmaids.

The chief bridesmaid will help you change into your going away clothes – usually about one hour after the speeches have ended, and you can take the opportunity to freshen up and apply a little extra make-up before returning to say your final good-byes to your parents and guests.

Just before you leave, you may like to toss your bouquet to one of the bridesmaids – or you could toss just one flower and keep the rest of the bouquet. There are no set rules, so this is one occasion when the bride can invent her own wedding "tradition".

THE MARRIAGE CEREMONY

BEFORE THE ceremony itself takes place, you will almost certainly have the opportunity to attend a rehearsal in the church. The minister will run through all the details of the service and explain the roles of each of the principal members of the wedding party.

It is best if the whole wedding party can attend the rehearsal, but if that is not possible it will help if the best man can be present so that he can later advise anyone who is unsure of the correct procedures.

CHURCH OF ENGLAND WEDDINGS

If you are getting married in an Anglican church, you should have already discussed with the minister whether the service is to be traditional or if it is to be conducted according to the increasingly popular modern form contained in the 1977 Alternative Service Book. The minister may have his own very definite opinions about this, but in fact both ceremonies are very moving.

Twenty minutes or so before the wedding is due to begin, the guests will start to arrive. The bride's family and friends are conducted to the left-hand seats of the church and the bridegroom's family and friends to those on the right-hand. The bridegroom and the best man are

45

seated at the top of the aisle. The bride's mother usually travels to the church with the bridesmaids, who remain in the church porch until the bride and her father arrive.

When the bride has taken her place at the church entrance, the organist will play the entrance music. At this point the congregation rise. The bride takes her father's right arm and they walk up the aisle followed by the bridesmaids. If it is a full choral service the minister may meet the bride in the porch and the procession will be led by the choir, followed by the minister, the bride and her father, and the bridesmaids.

The bridegroom and the best man meet the party at the chancel steps. The bride stands on the left of the bridegroom, and her father to her left, but slightly to the rear. The best man positions himself on the right of the bridegroom and, like the father, slightly to the rear. (After the bride's father has given away his daughter he can take his seat next to his wife in the front pew. The best man can also step to one side after he has presented the ring.)

At this point the chief bridesmaid steps forward to take the bride's bouquet or, if there are no bridesmaids, it may be handed to her father, who in turn may give it to his wife. The bouquet should be returned to the bride before she leaves the church – usually at the signing of the register.

The ceremony then begins. The minister first explains the significance of marriage according to the Scriptures. He then calls on the congregation – and the bride and bridegroom – to declare if there is any reason why the couple may not lawfully marry.

The minister then asks each of the couple in turn whether they promise to love, comfort, honour and forsaking all others (in the modern version) protect the other . . .

46

"as long as you both shall live:" to which they reply, "I will".

The bridegroom takes the bride's right hand in his, and they exchange vows; "to have and to hold, from this day forward; for better, for worse, for richer, for poorer, in sickness and in health, to love and to cherish, till death us do part."

The best man gives the ring to the minister, and the bridegroom places it on the third finger of the bride's left hand – or sometimes rings are exchanged. The bridegroom then makes his promise to the bride, in the modern version as follows:

> "I give you this ring
> as a sign of our marriage.
> With my body I honour you,
> all that I am I give to you,
> and all that I have I share with you,
> within the love of God,
> Father, Son and Holy Spirit."

The bride responds with the same promise, beginning "I receive this ring . . ." and the minister then pronounces them man and wife. After the marriage, and before signing the register, the minister will sometimes give a short address, especially if one or both of the married couple are known to him.

When the service is concluded, the wedding party move into the vestry to sign the register. The best man and the chief bridesmaid usually act as the two witnesses. Everyone has a chance to relax now, and one or two photographs are usually taken at the signing.

Coming out of the church, the bride takes the left arm of

the bridegroom and they are followed by any small bridesmaids; the chief bridesmaid and the best man; the bride's mother and the bridegroom's father; the bridegroom's mother and the bride's father; and the bridesmaids, often escorted by the ushers. Relatives leave next and are followed by special guests and then friends.

Outside, there will be a good deal of milling around as the wedding photographs are taken. Confetti (if it is permitted) will most likely be thrown when the bride and bridegroom decide it is time to leave for the reception.

QUAKER WEDDINGS

When a wedding is to take place according to the usages of the Society of Friends, the arrangements come under the care of the Society's registering officer for the area concerned.

It should be noted that besides giving notice to the registering officer, notice must also be given to the local Superintendant Registrar in the usual way.

The Society's registering officer will ensure that the Quaker regulations are followed and that, if they are satisfactorily completed, the meeting for worship to solemnise the marriage is duly approved.

At the ceremony, the usual custom is for the bride and bridegroom to sit surrounded by their relations and friends, and then for the two to stand at a moment when they feel it is right. Holding hands, the man makes the following declaration:

"Friends, I take this, my friend, ..., to be my wife, promising, through Divine assistance, to be

48

unto her a loving and faithful husband so long as we both on Earth shall live."

A certificate is then signed by the couple and two witnesses, stating that the couple made the necessary declaration, that they fulfilled the legal obligations and were duly married. All those present are invited to sign the certificate after the meeting is over.

No ring need appear at the ceremony, but sometimes one ring is given or rings may be exchanged after the declaration.

ROMAN CATHOLIC WEDDINGS

As with all marriages outside the Church of England, the couple must give notice of their intention to marry to the local Superintendent Registrar (or registrars if they live in different districts). Often the priest or one of his parishioners will be authorised to register the marriage, in which case the registrar is not required to be present at the wedding.

The marriage ceremony may be conducted during Mass (called a Nuptial Mass) or outside Mass – usually when one of the couple is not a Roman Catholic. However, the rite of marriage is the same in either case.

The priest first addresses the bride and bridegroom on the significance of marriage within the Church: it is regarded as a sacrament which will "enrich and strengthen" them so that the union will be one of "mutual and lasting fidelity".

The couple have to declare no lawful impediment to marriage; they promise to be faithful to each other and to accept and bring up children within the Roman Catholic faith. The priest invites them to declare their consent to marry "according to the rite of our holy Mother the Church" to which each replies "I will".

Right hands joined, the couple then call upon the congregation to witness the marriage, and make their vows, "to have and to hold from this day forward . . . till death do us part".

The priest confirms them in marriage and the rings are blessed and exchanged – or only one may be given – using the following words:

> "(Christian name only) take this ring as a sign
> of my love and fidelity. In the name of the
> Father and of the Son and of the Holy Spirit."

JEWISH WEDDINGS

When Jewish people marry, they are required to give notice to the registrar, but the marriage may be solemnized in a synagogue or private house. When a synagogue or house is used, the secretary of the synagogue to which the man belongs must take down the necessary particulars.

The ceremony, when held in a synagogue, varies in the form it takes. At the United Synagogue, the service is very ancient and interesting. The bride and bridegroom stand under a canopy – a *chuppah* – which is a reminder of the time when the Israelites were forced to live in tents. The couple's parents join in the ceremony by standing under the canopy with them and supporting them. Behind are their relations and friends.

50

The rabbi delivers a short address to the couple. Then the bridegroom turns to the bride and before placing the ring on her finger he says: "Behold, thou art consecrated unto me by this ring, according to the law of Moses and Israel."

The next step is the reading and signing of the Hebrew marriage contract. The man promises to be a true and faithful husband, and to protect, support, love, honour and cherish his bride. She promises to be true and faithful and to love, honour and cherish him.

Following the vows, the Seven Benedictions are recited and the couple drink wine, twice, from the same vessel; then the bridegroom dashes the glass to the ground. Drinking the wine reminds the couple that they are required to share each other's pleasures and halve each other's troubles. The broken glass symbolizes the weakness of marriage without love.

Before the ceremony is concluded, the following convenant is signed:

On the . . . day of the week, the . . . day of the month of . . . in the year . . . corresponding to the . . . of . . ., the Holy covenant of marriage was entered into, in . . ., between the bridegroom, . . ., and his bride, . . .

The said bridegroom made the following declaration to his bride: "Be thou my wife according to the Law of Moses and of Israel. I faithfully promise that I will be a true husband unto thee. I will honour and cherish thee; I will work for thee; I will protect and support thee; and will provide all that is necessary for thy due sustenance, even as it beseemeth a Jewish husband to do. I also take upon myself all such further obligations for thy maintenance during thy lifetime as are prescribed by our religious statutes."

And the said bride plighted her troth unto him, in affection and with sincerity, and has thus taken upon herself the fulfilment of all the duties incumbent upon a Jewish wife.

This covenant of marriage was duly executed and witnessed this day according to the usage of Israel.

THE RECEPTION

THE RECEPTION may be formal or informal, depending on the type of wedding, the number of guests and personal preference. Usually, a formal reception is held in a hotel, where facilities and staff can be laid on for a full sit-down meal – the "wedding breakfast". A buffet reception can be a less expensive option.

Alternatively, a reception could be held at the bride's parents' home – if enough people can be found to help with the catering! Another arrangement is to hold a meal in a restaurant for just a few close relatives and friends. In the evening, a party – perhaps with a buffet – can be staged for the other guests – as well as friends who may not have attended the ceremony. You may want to arrange to pay for drinks at the bar for a short time and at some point in the celebrations there is bound to be a toast to the bride and bridegroom.

However, if you plan to have a reception or party of any kind in a hotel or function room, the booking should be made well in advance. Start looking two or three months before the wedding (earlier if possible), compare costs and menus and check on parking facilities.

Outside caterers come into their own when the reception is held at the bride's parents' home, or in a hall specially hired for the occasion. Again these arrangements will have to be made in good time.

A Formal Reception

A formal or semi-formal reception, will have a receiving line to welcome the guests. This usually consists of the bride's mother and father, the bridegroom's mother and father and the bride and bridegroom themselves – in that order. If a large number of guests has been invited and you want to speed proceedings up, the bride and bridegroom can do the receiving on their own.

On entering, the guests are usually presented with a glass of wine or an aperitif, and when the last guest has been received everyone looks for their name card and takes their place at the tables. Sometimes seating arrangements are left to the guests to make their own choices. If there are separate bar and dining areas, early arrivals can wait comfortably in the bar until everyone is assembled.

Seating arrangements vary according to the number of guests and the layout of the tables. For a formal reception, however, there will be a "top table" for the principal members of the wedding party and the attendants (see diagram on page 123). Since it is an honour to sit at the top table, be careful not to hurt anyone's feelings by including a guest who is not also a member of the wedding party. An aunt who has flown in from Australia for the wedding may, however, be classed as an exception!

The bride and the two mothers usually work out how best to seat the other guests. You will probably want to aim at some interchange between the families – but not so much that no-one knows what to say to each other.

After the last course is completed (or alternatively, about halfway through the proceedings) the cake-cutting ceremony and the toasts and speeches take place.

The first to speak is the bride's father who stands and

says a few words before proposing the main toast: "Health and happiness to the bride and bridegroom." The bridegroom responds briefly, thanking the bride's parents and the guests, and ends by proposing a toast to the health of the bridesmaids. The best man follows by replying for the bridesmaids and reading out the congratulatory telegrams. The bride may also elect to say a few words.

All the speeches should be kept short and informal. If they can be witty without being offensive, so much the better. However, a sincere approach often goes down just as well, so if you have any doubts about your abilities as a humorist, it is best not to try.

The cake should have been ordered some weeks before and delivered to the reception on the day of the wedding. Icing on a traditional wedding cake can be very thick so it will help if this is already cut through. The bride holds the knife in her right hand, with the bridegroom's right hand on hers, and her left hand on top. After the first slice has been successfully dealt with, the cake can be taken away and cut into smaller pieces for the guests to eat with their coffee. You may wish to rescue the top tier to keep for a christening. Use cake boxes to send pieces of the cake to people who could not attend the wedding.

If there is to be dancing, the bride and bridegroom will be first on to the floor, followed by the chief bridesmaid and the best man, and members of the two families.

After a while spent chatting to the guests, the couple slip away to change into going-away clothes, returning for a few minutes to say their final good-byes before going on honeymoon. Traditionally, just before they leave, the bride tosses her bouquet to a bridesmaid or a female guest who, tradition has it, will be the next in line for marriage.

THE ROLE OF THE BEST MAN

INFORMATION and organisation are the key words for anyone called upon to perform the duties of the best man. Although nominally no more than a friend and supporter of the bridegroom, he is also, in reality, expected to be a planner, trouble-shooter and "fixer" – the person people turn to automatically for advice or assistance. The best man should also be dependable, for much of the smooth-running of the wedding is his responsibility. Beyond that, however, there is no reason why anyone who is prepared to devote some time and effort to the role should not cope successfully with the role.

If you are to be best man at a wedding, the first thing to do is to find out as much as possible about the wedding itself: times, dates and addresses are most important, as are the names of all the other members of the wedding party. Since the best man is generally responsible for transport, you should check on parking facilities both at the church and the reception (probably the largest single source of questions from the guests). Write all the information down as soon as you get it.

The best man has several specific duties to carry out, which should be committed to memory; it is no good remembering the name of the bride's second cousin while failing to produce the ring on cue. The major areas of responsibility can be broken down as follows:

The Ushers Help the bridegroom to choose them and see that each knows what his duties are. Usually, at the ceremony, the chief usher will show the bride's mother and the bridegroom's parents to their seats: the others stand at strategic points along the aisle to show the guests to their seats (bride's family and friends on the left; bridegroom's family and friends on the right), and there will be Order of Service sheets and/or hymn books to be handed out.

The Stag Party Persuade the bridegroom to hold the party a couple of days before the ceremony. Help to organise the party, and don't let the bridegroom drive!

The Ring At the church, keep it handy and offer it to the minister at the appropriate time. Carry a cheap substitute, just in case (a curtain ring will do).

Transport The best man arranges cars to the church for the bridegroom and himself; and cars to the reception for the bride and bridegroom, the bridesmaids and himself. Draw up a list of taxi telephone numbers in case you break down on the way to the church. Arrange for the bridegroom's car to be parked at the reception if it is to be used for the honeymoon; if not, alternative travel arrangements will have to be made. Make sure that all the guests have transport to the reception.

The Speech Make a brief speech at the reception in reply to the toast to the bridesmaids. (See the chapter on Toasts and Speeches.)

A day or two before the wedding, also check that all the other arrangements are running to plan – especially where the bridegroom is concerned. Here's a list of the sort of things to check:

(i) Have the buttonholes been ordered? Who is collecting/delivering them?

(ii) Have the hired suits been collected by everyone concerned?

(iii) Are all the documents in order – banns certificate, travel tickets, passports, driving licence, travellers cheques, hotel reservations, etc?

(iv) When has the minister requested that the fees be paid?

On the wedding day, just before setting off with the bridegroom, check that the following are accounted for: the ring, buttonholes, driving licence, travel documents, the banns certificate, taxi telephone numbers, honeymoon luggage (bride's and bridegroom's), going-away clothes (in a separate case), Order of Service sheets, telegrams (if the bride's mother is not bringing them) and money.

Get the bridegroom to the church at least fifteen minutes before the bride is due – taking traffic problems into account when planning the journey time.

At the reception, take charge of any late wedding presents and help to transport these, and if there is to be a display the other gifts, to the bride's parents' home. Also collect and return the bridegroom's wedding suit if it is hired.

JUST RETURNING THE SUIT!

THE ROLE OF THE CHIEF BRIDESMAID

THE CHIEF bridesmaid, usually a sister or close friend of the bride, acts as adviser, messenger and general assistant to the bride in much the same way as the best man does for the bridegroom. Although she is not so concerned with making arrangements for the day, she will be expected to help the bride in any way she can before the wedding and wait on her during the ceremony. She also looks after the other bridesmaids – especially the young ones.

Her main duties are as follows:

(i) She may help the bride to choose the wedding dress and those of the bridesmaids and also the bride's trousseau.

(ii) On the wedding day, she may help the bride to dress, although she will leave for the church before the bride.

(iii) At the church, she makes sure the bride's dress and veil are arranged neatly; she follows behind the bride and her father in the procession and takes the bouquet from the bride when they reach the chancel steps.

(iv) When the bride and bridegroom move into the vestry to sign the register, she follows on the arm of the best man, before the parents and near

59

relations, and may be asked to be a witness at the signing of the register.

(v) During the recessional music, she leaves on the arm of the best man.

(vi) At the reception, she generally assists the bride, and helps her to change into her going-away clothes.

I AM GENERAL ASSISTANT

I AM GENERAL DOGS-BODY

TOASTS AND SPEECHES

I F YOU are one of the lucky few expected to "say a few words" at the wedding reception – don't worry! You will not have to speak for very long (four minutes is ample) nor astound everybody with your wit and eloquence. A few simple, sincere and, if possible, entertaining remarks are all that are called for and, with a little thought, that should not prove too difficult. If, however you do find yourself in difficulty, a copy of *Wedding Speeches & Toasts* by Barbara Jeffery ought to bring you more confidence.

What to Say
Most speeches at a wedding have a purpose: they either propose a toast, or reply to a toast. That in itself will suggest much of what you say, since you will either be paying compliments, or thanking people for their kind remarks. However, you will want to put this fluently and in your own words, and to do that, you will need to consider your material.

It is not a good idea to simply learn a speech from a book, because it will not be *you* speaking and you will end up sounding contrived. The sincere speech is what people want to hear.

A good way to prepare a speech is to note down ideas and thoughts as they come to you – your first impression of the bridegroom, perhaps, or a reason why the couple are particularly suited. Don't worry about the exact wording or form of the speech yet; that comes later, when you have a list of ideas from which to choose.

If you like, include some quotations – about marriage, happiness or weddings. Use them as pegs for your own ideas. The following examples may start you thinking:

> "Marriage is a wonderful institution, but who wants to live in an institution?" (*Groucho Marx*)

> "Marriage is a sort of friendship recognised by the police." (*Anon*)

> "Man's best possession is a sympathetic wife." (*William Congreve*)

> "For in what stupid age or nation,
> Was marriage ever out of fashion?" (*Samuel Butler*)

> "He's the most married man I ever saw." (*Artemus Ward*)

> "Love and murder will out." (*William Congreve*)

> 'I have always thought that every woman should marry, and no man." (*Benjamin Disraeli*)

Jokes also have a place in wedding speeches; however, if they're of the "funny story" type, one is usually enough. Vulgar or "blue" jokes are a sure way to ruin any reception, so leave them out!

Once you have your thoughts on paper, the next stage is to work out the form of the speech – how you are going to open, what your main theme(s) will be, the people you must remember to mention or thank in the speech and how you are going to round it off. Decide which ideas are best and see if they can be linked without too much contortion (the phrase "talking about . . . reminds me of . . ." will soon have the audience yawning). You will probably end up with just a few ideas that you feel comfortable with – and that is plenty! For the best man's speech, a few amusing anecdotal stories about the groom often go down well, but should not make reference to past flames!

Sometimes the most difficult part of preparing a speech is knowing how to begin. You don't want to plunge immediately into your main themes or say anything too serious just yet. If you really cannot think of a suitable opening, a comment about the speech you have just heard, or the inadequacies of the one you are about to deliver, will usually do the trick.

To sum up, then: your speech should be brief, fluent, and sincere, and it should fulfill its purpose of proposing or replying to a toast.

How to Say It

No matter how well chosen your words may be or how comfortable you feel with them, they will be largely wasted if you do not get them across coherently and naturally.

Again, a lot depends on preparation. You should familiarise yourself with the speech so that you don't have to read it out word for word: if you do, you will lose all sense of contact with the audience and appear nervous and insincere. What you *can* do is to write down the main points or headings on one or two cards which you can then refer to during the speech. Even if you remember it all, the fact that there is a prompt ready, just in case, will boost your confidence.

Since you are addressing the whole room, you will have

to speak louder than usual in order to be heard. This can be a problem. It is not easy to speak loudly, yet naturally. Try to imagine that you are talking or conversing with the audience; not lecturing or bawling at them. Speak quite slowly and deliberately so that they can follow you without concentrating too hard. If you have an accent, it is silly to try to disguise it. It just puts an added strain on you and usually fools nobody.

Avoid, if possible, shuffling your feet, swaying from side to side, constantly adjusting your tie, or jingling change in your pockets. All of these are distracting, and usually indicate that the speaker is nervous and ill-at-ease. Try to stand and act as you would in any ordinary conversation. If you're worried about what to do with your hands, the answer is, whatever you normally do. Prompt cards will give you something to hold, and there's nothing to stop you putting your hands in your pockets – as long as you don't keep pulling them out every time you want to make a point.

When you talk to people, you also have to look at them. There is no clearer sign of tension than the speaker who stares fixedly at a point on the opposite wall. You don't, of course, have to swivel your eyes frantically in an effort to take in everybody at once. Let your eyes rest gradually on different sections of the audience, and when you mention someone by name, turn to look at them.

Remember, appearing to be natural and relaxed – even if you are not – is the sign of a good speaker.

The Rehearsal
Once you have the speech fairly well worked out, run through it a few times, by yourself, in front of a mirror.

Now is the time to practise using a raised voice. You will probably find yourself pausing for breath more often than you thought. This will affect your phrasing and you may have to alter and/or shorten some sentences that do not sound quite right. Watch out for irritating gestures in the mirror.

It is, in fact, much more satisfying to speak before a live audience than in front of an unresponsive mirror. If you are happy with the rehearsal, you should have no difficulty when your turn comes to take the floor at the reception.

Points to Remember

(i)   Prepare a speech that will suit the occasion (at an informal reception you may only be required to propose a toast – if even that).

(ii)   Ask yourself what the guests would like to hear. What would *you* like to hear in their position?

(iii   Don't forget to propose or respond to a toast if that is the purpose of the speech.

(iv)   Keep it short; three to five minutes is quite enough.

(v)   Don't use "blue" jokes.

(vi)   Don't get drunk before you speak.

(vii)   Speak in a raised voice but don't shout.

(viii) Avoid long, complicated sentences that are difficult to follow.

(ix)   Be yourself.

As a final check, here's a run down of the major points that would normally be covered by each speaker:

The *bride's father* – or uncle, family friend, etc. – talks affectionately about the bride and bridegroom, offers a few thoughts of his own about love/marriage, and ends by proposing the toast to the bride and bridegroom.

The *bridegroom* tells everyone how fortunate he is to have married such a wonderful bride. He thanks the bride's parents – for their daughter's hand and for the reception – and the guests – for their presents and for attending the wedding. He acknowledges the invaluable services of the best man, and he proposes a toast to the bridesmaids.

The *best man* replies for the bridesmaids, thanking the bridegroom for the toast, and adds a few complimentary comments of his own. He congratulates the bridegroom on his good luck, and wishes the couple happiness in the future. He concludes by reading the telegrams.

AND NOW A TOAST...
TO THE BRIDESMAIDS!

THE SECOND MARRIAGE

THE MAIN difference between a first and second marriage – especially when both parties are divorced – is that the second is usually a much less formal affair.

The bride and bridegroom normally send out invitations in their own name, whether or not they will be hosting the reception. The wording might be:

Patricia and Robert have much pleasure in inviting you to their wedding at All Saints Church, Kingsgrove, on Saturday 27th April at 2.45 pm (and afterwards to a reception at The Bell Inn, Kingsgrove).

Should the bride's parents wish to give the reception, they can send out separate informal invitations:

We are very pleased to invite you to a reception at The Bell Inn, Kingsgrove, following our daughter Patricia's marriage to Robert Brown at All Saints Church on Saturday 27th April.

Guests are likely to be friends and immediate relations: elaborate family "do's" are not expected (you can catch up on all the other relations at a later time). A second wedding when the bride or bridegroom has been divorced is generally not the place to renew acquaintances with former in-laws.

The bride, if she is divorced or a widow, does not normally wear a white wedding dress or veil, but she will want to wear something special just the same. A well-cut suit or long silk dress are often chosen, both for civil and church weddings (many Non-conformist denominations will allow a second marriage ceremony to take place in church). If it is the bride's first marriage, she may wear whatever she likes.

There are no rules about giving the reception, although it is usually a more relaxed occasion than the traditional formal reception. You could invite friends to a restaurant after the ceremony, have a cocktail party in a hotel, or throw a party or disco in the evening. You will probably want to keep the tone fairly lighthearted – and that applies to the speeches, too, if there are to be any. Often, the toast to the bride and bridegroom is proposed by an old and/or mutual friend.

If you can, arrange to have a honeymoon after the wedding. It will give you a chance to relax and enjoy each other's company away from the pressures of home – or children, if there are any from a previous marriage. Starting off with just the two of you together underlines the special nature of your relationship, and helps to make the wedding even more of an occasion to remember.

A DIVORCE IN THE FAMILY

If the parents of either the bride or the bridegroom are divorced, a little tact and cooperation all round will help to ensure that the wedding is still a happy occasion – both for them, and for the couple about to be married.

At the church and the reception, the seating arrangements are slightly altered. If the bride's parents are divorced, then her mother will be shown to the first pew on the left hand side of the church. She may be with her new husband, or, if she has not remarried, with a close relative. The bride's father takes his seat in the second or third pew, also with his new partner if he has remarried. The same arrangements apply to the bridegroom's parents if they are divorced.

At the reception, the receiving line includes the bridegroom's mother and father, and whoever is giving the reception – usually the bride's own mother and father. This applies whether or not either of the parents are divorced. New partners are not normally included in the receiving line.

Seating arrangements at the top table should be discussed with all the parties concerned. Depending on how cooperative they are determined to be, there should be no problem in finding everyone a place. (One possible arrangement is shown on page 123).

If the bride's parents are divorced and she has been brought up by her mother and a stepfather, he may be asked to make the first speech and propose the main toast. However, the exact arrangements will vary according to the individual circumstances and should be discussed and agreed beforehand.

The most important thing is that personal feelings about ex-partners do not get out of hand and interfere with the success of the wedding – and if the situation is handled with dignity and understanding, there is no reason why they should.

CHANGING YOUR NAME

YOU DO not have to change your name when you get married, although it is generally expected and usually makes life a little easier when you're making joint arrangements of a social or legal nature.

Sometimes a woman retains her maiden name for business purposes, when to change it would be inconvenient or potentially damaging. Having two separate identities is confusing, but it may be the best solution in the circumstances.

If you do decide to change your name, however, there are lots of people who will want to know about it. It may take a little time to get round all the relevant authorities and organisations, but here are some of the more important ones to note:

Employer, bank, building society, post office (or any other organisation with whom you have a savings account), insurance companies, credit card companies, passport office (you don't have to change the name on your passport but it is usually more convenient if you do), Inland Revenue, Department of Health and Social Security, Driver and Vehicle Licensing Centre (for change of driver's licence and vehicle registration documents), your doctor and your dentist.

If you are going abroad on honeymoon and you want a new passport in your married name, you will have to apply to the Passport Office, Clive House, Petty France, London SW1. You will not receive the passport until you are legally married, but it may be sent to the appropriate minister or registrar to give to you after the wedding.

MAY I SPEAK TO
MISS FROBISHER PLEASE

THE HONEYMOON

I F THE wedding ceremony and reception need careful thought and planning, so does the first trip that the bride and bridegroom take together as a married couple. Most people will want to have a honeymoon, and the tradition of starting on the honeymoon immediately after the wedding is still followed by the majority of couples who get married today.

Apart from the question of cost, the most important factor is to take a honeymoon which will appeal to both of you. A honeymoon in which the interests of one partner are followed while the other trails along with little enthusiasm is hardly the best way to start married life. So there should be a discussion well before the wedding: read through the brochures together, and book the holiday well in advance.

When you're thinking about where to go for the honeymoon, remember to take into account the date of the wedding. If you're getting married in the winter months, and you want sun, you will have to pay for it. Alternatively, you could opt for a honeymoon in a city like London or Paris, where the attractions are not so dependent on the weather.

Don't be shy about admitting your new status: some travel firms offer honeymoon trips complete with free champagne and four poster beds, and hotels will often make a special effort to see that the honeymoon stay is as enjoyable as possible.

Honeymoons abroad also mean you have to check on passports, travel tickets, travellers cheques, hotel reservations, foreign currency and medical insurance, as well as any inoculations that may be required. Don't leave it to the last minute. You will have enough to do in the run up to the wedding without worrying about the possible after effects of an injection against cholera!

Finally, don't be too surprised if the honeymoon doesn't live up to *all* your expectations. The first few weeks of marriage are rarely without their problems. Two adults who have already developed personalities and ways of their own have to learn to adjust to one another. Relax, take things as they come, and you will soon find yourself looking back with affection on what will almost certainly be one of the most memorable holidays of your life.

JUST RELAX
AND LEARN TO
ADJUST

FINANCING A HAPPY MARRIAGE

MONEY IS the root of all evil – so the old saying goes – and it is certainly true that many marriages come to grief over it. When you're planning your wedding day it is very easy to be over-confident that you'll live happily ever after. But unless you have a Fairy Godmother it would be sheer folly not to look ahead to financial realities of your future. You should talk frankly about your attitudes towards money, work and material needs *before* your wedding, so there will be no misunderstandings about what you each expect from, and hope to contribute to, the financial side of your marriage.

You will probably know whether you both intend to go on working – at least for the time being – but deciding where to live and how to afford all you will need for your new home may be harder. Just as important, though perhaps less obvious, are decisions about joint budgeting; how to run your home and still have enough money left to enjoy yourselves. However, with a bit of forethought, trust and organisation you will not only both be clear about what lies ahead, you should also avoid some of the pitfalls which part the inexperienced or unwary from their money.

Setting up a new home is always expensive, so don't let any of your hard earned income go to the tax inspector unnecessarily. Write and tell him as soon as you get married, and if either of you stops work send him the P45 form which your employer must give you. Keeping the tax-man informed – of mortgages and babies too – will ensure you get any rebates due. The same applies to the Social Security Office if you get any benefits.

Your first big decision will be where to live. If you have very little money you will have to rent or live with family or friends. But with luck you may have enough to think of buying a house or flat. Remember that besides the purchase price itself, you will need to pay a solicitor, surveyor, Land Registry fees and maybe Stamp Duty. If you think you can afford all this, consider the cost of essential repairs and decoration, and don't forget to look at the likely cost of fuel, rates and insurance before you finally go ahead and buy.

After the building itself, your next big expense will be decorating and furnishing. Start before your wedding day by including things you will need on a wedding present list.

However generous your friends and relatives, you will probably have to buy some large items yourselves – but remember that you don't really *need* every home comfort from the start! You can also save quite a lot by taking on a home that needs some repairs or redecoration, particularly if you do them yourselves – which can also be very satisfying.

One thing you must do, however, is to insure the contents of your home against theft, loss or damage. The way you assess the value of the contents will depend on the type of policy you choose – indemnity or "new for old" – but in either case, the cost is not great in relation to the potential benefits, and your own peace of mind!

If you are renting, you should not sign any agreement without a careful look at the financial implications. Be certain you can really afford the rent – and that it is reasonable. Check whether you qualify for a rent or rate rebate, and make sure you know who is responsible for repairs and insurance – an unexpected bill can really throw you if your finances are already stretched.

Planning Your Budget

Your financial situation will probably be quite different after the wedding. There may be bills for rates, insurance, etc. that you haven't faced before, and if you're not used to running a home, you may be amazed how the cost of soap and light bulbs adds up. So, to make sure your money goes where it's most needed, start by adding up the big bills you expect to pay over the year, and then average them over twelve months. If there's nothing left for day to day spending, you will have to change your lifestyle.

Assuming there is more than this, it is a good idea to keep a full diary of how you spend your money over a couple of months – not immediately after the wedding, though, when it may be extra high. This is not in order to spy on each other! In fact you should try to have some money each (even if it's only a small amount) to spend on whatever you fancy. But now, as a couple, the bulk of your money will go on things you both want, and the only way to be certain where the money goes is to write it down. Then, if things get tight, you can work out where savings can best be made, rather than argue pointlessly.

How you apportion your financial responsibilities is a matter of personal choice – many couples open a joint bank account when they marry while others arrange that the husband pays all the bills and the wife deals with daily expenses. The actual method you choose isn't important, so long as it's fair and you both understand what your responsibilities are. Also, see your bank manager about operating a budget account for recurring bills – it will mean you can meet your bills more easily.

If you think you can save anything, decide first what you are saving for – a house, a holiday, a car – and then look for the savings scheme that will best suit your needs. Even if you have very little to spare, do try to build up a few savings just in case an emergency arises.

The Moneylenders
While setting up your home, you may be tempted to borrow money. Borrowing can be helpful, but must always be approached with caution. Advertisements may lead you to believe that borrowing will solve all your problems; but you can be certain that anyone lending you money will be making a profit – out of your pocket. Before you borrow cash, or buy goods on credit, always make sure you know how much you will have to pay *in total*, and be realistic about whether you can afford it.

If you want to borrow, start with the cheapest lenders – the building societies and banks. You may be able to increase your mortgage to finance certain home improvements, but for most purchases a bank loan will be the answer. If you haven't already got a bank account your marriage is a good time to open one, and it is anyway a good time to go to see your bank manager. He will be able to advise you which type of loan would suit you best, and also which sorts of bank account you can have.

Credit cards are increasingly used, and if you repay your debt in full each month they are a good – and generally free – way of ironing out your spending peaks. However, for longer term borrowing they can be expensive.

If you run into trouble with meeting the instalments on any loan, tell the lender at once. Any reputable one will try to come to a mutually satisfactory arrangement. Far better, however, is to avoid trouble in the first place by being fully aware of your financial situation and not taking on more than you can afford. The only way to do this is to organise your budget carefully .

Financial management can be a complicated business, but there are plenty of good books and expert people who can be a great help to you – never be shy of asking.

BUYING A HOUSE

FROM NECESSITY or choice, many couples live happily in rented houses or flats. Others prefer to own their houses, and it is for them that this chapter is written.

If you are going to take out a mortgage, you must answer two financial questions: how much capital can you put down, and how much do you expect to be able to pay regularly out of your future income?

Unless you are a "sitting tenant" you are very unlikely to get a mortgage of more than 95 per cent of the purchase price, and probably it will be less. You will have to pay the balance yourself. You will also have various legal expenses, and all the costs of furnishing and decorating. Altogether you should assume that you will have to find *at least* ten per cent of the purchase price, in ready cash.

The amount you borrow will have to be repaid in regular instalments; and your future outgoings will also include ground rent (if the house is leasehold), general and water rates, insurance premiums, and the cost of maintenance and repairs. The total of these expenses should not usually be more than a quarter of your basic income; in other words, one week's earnings should cover one month's outgoings on the cost of the house.

How to Raise the Money
The chief lenders of money for house purchase are build-

ing societies, local authorities, banks, and assurance (or insurance) companies. You may also get help from mortgage brokers, who sometimes have access to other funds – but you may have to pay more than the usual rates.

Most house purchasers borrow from *building societies*. Normally you will be able to borrow up to eighty per cent of the society's valuation of the property, but if it is old or in a poor state of repair you may not get so much – in fact, you may be turned down altogether unless you undertake to do certain repairs within a given period of time. It is possible to get a larger percentage loan in some cases, but you will almost certainly be asked to take out an insurance policy to cover the extra. The cost can be added on to your loan so that you pay it back by instalments, along with your mortgage repayments.

Apart from the value of the house, the other factor to be taken into account in determining how much you will be able to borrow is your financial status. If you are both earning, you will probably be able to borrow two-and-a-half times the larger salary (pre-tax) plus an amount which is equal to the lower; if only one of you is earning you will only get two-and-a-half times that salary. However, societies do vary on exactly how they make these calculations, so it may be worth asking around to get the best deal.

In order to stand the best possible chance of getting a mortgage, you should try to save with the building society (or more than one) for some time *before* you ask for a loan. Even if you can't afford much, they will probably think better of you if you have been a regular saver. Moreover, if you save through the "Homeloan Scheme" you could actually get a grant from the government to buy your first home. You have to keep a few hundred pounds on your "Homeloan" account for a year before getting the grant, but many couples need to save for longer than that to buy a house anyway, so it is certainly worth asking for details. (The scheme is also run through banks, Trustee and National Savings Banks, the National Girobank and the Ulster Savings Bank, so you can put your savings with whoever you think you will be trying to get a loan from in the future.)

Only a very small percentage of mortgages are from *local authorities*, but they are often especially useful to young couples because councils are more likely than building societies to lend money for older properties and converted flats. They are also more likely to lend you a bigger proportion of the price, and may even lend the whole of it. If you want to try for a council mortgage, ask for details at the Town Hall. You will be more likely to get a mortgage if you have lived in the area for some time, but this is not a necessary condition. When money is scarce with the building societies, you may stand a better chance with the council. When building societies have plenty of money you can still gain the benefits of a council mortgage even though the loan may come through a building society; this is because there is an arrangement whereby mortgages with local council specifications are given by building societies to people nominated by the council.

As with any loan agreement you should make quite sure you understand what your repayments will be on a council mortgage – the interest may be different from that charged by a building society.

A comparatively recent innovation in the mortgage market is the growth of *bank mortgages*. Banks have long been, and still are, a useful source of bridging loans to help you over the period between buying one house and selling another. They can also help with topping up a building society mortgage that is not quite big enough. Besides these facilities, banks are now offering mortgages in just the same way as building societies and local authorities. If you have had a healthy bank account for some time, it might be a good place to go for your mortgage.

There are other lenders, too. Insurance companies and finance houses may be useful, and some solicitors have access to trust funds for investment purposes. The problem with all these is finding out about them, and here a mortgage broker may be able to help. Friends, relatives, and even the person you are buying the house from, may be willing to lend you at least some of the money you need. Such arrangements can work very well, but you must be even more careful than with the better established mortgage lenders. First and foremost, get a written agreement, drawn up by a solicitor. Make absolutely sure that you understand the terms of the agreement, and always get a solicitor of your own to look over it. If you get a mortgage from a private person, make sure that you get the appropriate forms signed each year to send to the income tax office for tax relief. Above all, remember that building societies, local authorities and banks have a great deal of experience in lending money. If none of them is prepared to lend to you, it just could be that you haven't really got the resources and prospects to cover the sort of loan you are looking for.

Types of Mortgages
Whether you borrow from a building society, local au-

thority or bank, you will have to decide what sort of mortgage you want.

The most common type is the *repayment mortgage*. You repay the loan in monthly instalments over, say, twenty-five years, each instalment being part interest and part repayment of the loan. You get tax relief on the interest part of each instalment. The relief will be greatest at the beginning of the period when the interest is at its highest.

If you don't pay tax, the tax relief on the interest element of a repayment mortgage will obviously be of no help to you, and in this situation you could choose to have an *option mortgage*. With this type, you pay a lower rate of interest, and the government makes up the difference to the building society.

You should take expert advice before deciding between a repayment or an option mortgage, because it is not easy to change during the course of a loan and a wrong decision could be to your disadvantage.

A third type of mortgage offered by most lenders – including some insurance companies – is the *endowment mortgage*. Instead of repaying your loan over the years, you pay only the interest on the loan, plus premiums for a life assurance policy which matures in a given number of years to repay the entire debt. You can also get a "with profits" endowment policy, which will leave you with a lump sum to spare on top of what is needed to repay your mortgage. However, for this you naturally have to pay a higher monthly instalment. Some "low cost" endowment policies are very good value, but you should nevertheless go carefully since if mortgage interest rates rise, you are far less likely than with an option or repayment mortgage to be allowed extra time to make the repayments; you will just have to find the extra cash from your budget.

An endowment mortgage has the advantage that, in the event of the policy holder's death, the life assurance element would repay the outstanding debt at any time. However, you can, and should, take out a quite cheap "term life assurance policy" to cover the repayment of any type of mortgage. Such a policy will not bring the profit of an endowment arrangement, but nor will you have the risk of any financial loss if you sell your house and redeem the mortgage before the end of the term – a point to watch for with any endowment scheme.

If you have a high enough income to be looking for the sort of long term investment offered by an endowment mortgage, you should also look at the many other investment schemes that are in no way linked to mortgages before making your final decision.

Old or New?

You will also have to consider whether to buy a new house or one that has already been occupied. Most modern houses are better insulated than older houses, and modern building materials are also generally superior. But some poor-quality housing continues to be built, and unless you know something about the subject, it is advisable, when buying a new house, to choose one that has been certified by the National House Building Council. The Council operates a protection scheme covering all houses put up by builders on its register. The scheme has limitations – storm damage and normal wear and tear are excluded – but if minor structural faults emerge within two years you can claim compensation; if there is subsidence or a major defect in the actual load bearing structure, you can claim up to ten years after the house was built. It is not a guarantee, but it does provide some assurance that the house has been well built. You can get details of the scheme from the Council at 365 Euston Road, London NW1.

If you decide to buy an older property, it is very important to have a proper structural survey carried out. The building society will have their own valuation survey done, but you cannot rely on this to reveal whether the house is in sound condition. You can often save money by asking the surveyor to do both surveys at the same time, and some building societies now offer this service as a matter of course.

There is one other method of choosing a house, and that is by having one built. Most of the big lenders grant building mortgages, the advances being made in instalments as the work proceeds. If you decide to do this, you should employ an architect to design the house and supervise its construction. If you cannot afford to do this you will probably be better off with a ready-built house put up by a builder on the NHBC register. You can get full information about architects' fees from the Royal Institute of British Architects, 66 Portland Place, London W1.

THERE APPEARS TO BE A DEFECT IN THE ACTUAL LOAD BEARING STRUCTURE

WEDDING SUPERSTITIONS

MOST OF us like to play the superstition game at one time or another and weddings in particular come in for a whole range of sayings and warnings – which are fun if you take them with "a pinch of salt"!

Choosing the right month can bring an extra share of luck. Take June for example. Apart from the fact that we normally have good weather, the popularity of this month is rooted in the fact that it is named after the goddess Juno, the adored and faithful wife of Jupiter, who is the protector of women and marriage, and is said to bestow especial blessings on those who wed in her month:

> Married in the month of roses – June
> Life will be one long honeymoon.

When it comes to deciding on the date it is unlucky to marry on your birthday; however it is particularly lucky if husband and wife share the same birthday although they must be a year or two apart.

There are many sayings intended for the bride. The need for her to wear "something old, something new, something borrowed and something blue" at the wedding is well known. It is generally considered unlucky for the bride to make her own dress – even professional dressmakers rarely do – and it is even more unlucky to try on the full bridal array too soon, especially if she sees herself in a full length mirror. She can, of course, leave off a glove or a shoe out of respect for the old tradition!

Did you know that an old veil is thought to be luckier than a new one? This is particularly true if borrowed from a woman who is happily married, or an heirloom of the bride's family. The good fortune and/or fertility of the earlier marriages passes with the veil to its new wearer.

The colour of the bride's dress is supposed to be a faithful portent of the future:

> White is a symbol of purity and of high virtues.
> Green typifies youth, hope and happiness.
> Red is a sign of vigour, courage and great passion. (There may be a touch of jealousy in its reading, however.)
> Violet denotes dignity, pride and a condition of high ideals.

The wedding procession is not overlooked. The bride must leave her home by the front door with her right foot foremost. It is considered lucky if the sun shines or she sees a rainbow on the way or meets a black cat or a chimney sweep 'in his blacks'.

The modern custom of sending a piece of wedding cake to friends and relatives not present has its roots in a desire for them to share its luck-bringing properties and one old saying advises the bride to keep a piece of the cake – if she does her husband will be faithful to her.

The following dates are reckoned to be especially lucky for weddings:

January	2	4	11	19	21
February	1	3	10	19	21
March	3	5	12	20	23
April	2	4	12	20	22
May	2	4	12	20	23
June	1	3	11	19	21
July	1	3	12	19	21	31
August	2	11	18	20	20
September	1	9	16	18	28
October			15	18	27	29
November	5	11	13	22	25
December	1	8	10	19	23	29

Other supersititions about the wedding day are of a more general nature.

- • "Happy the bride whom the sun shines on" may be a well-known saying. But did you know that one way to guard against rain is to feed your cat on the morning of the wedding? (If you're getting married in Germany – steer clear of cats. Each drop of rain is looked upon as a blessing on the marriage.)

- • It is a good sign if the bride is awakened on the day by the song of a bird – and also if she discovers a spider in the folds of her dress!

- • It's bad luck to break anything – especially a mirror – on the wedding morning, or to lose the heel of a shoe.

- With each glance in the mirror, the bride is supposed to add something to her make-up or clothing – even if it's only a pair of gloves.

- It's bad luck for the couple to meet in the morning before the wedding – but good luck if they smile at each other when they meet in the church.

- A bride is not supposed to weep before the marriage, but she may do so as much as she likes afterwards: this proves that she is not a witch, who could shed only three tears from her left eye.

- If the bride sees a lamb, a dove, a spider, a toad, or a black cat on her way to the church, it is a sign of good luck; but it is reckoned as a very bad omen if she should encounter a funeral party, or if a pig crosses the road in front of the wedding car.

The Bridegroom

Rather fewer superstitions surround the conduct of the bridegroom on his wedding day. All will be well so long as he does not see his bride in her wedding dress before he meets her in the church and does not drop the ring before putting it on the bride's finger. If she has to assist him in this, he may expect to be ruled by her in the future. He should pay the church fees (through the best man) with an odd sum of money, carry a small mascot in his pocket, and on no account turn back for anything after leaving for the church.

After the honeymoon, the husband should carry his wife over the threshold of their new home. When this is done, both will be rewarded with all the good fortune they could wish for.

WEDDING ANNIVERSARIES

MOST PEOPLE like to celebrate wedding anniversaries with presents and perhaps have an evening out at a favourite restaurant or theatre.

Traditionally, certain materials are associated with individual years in the marriage series, the idea being that anniversary presents in those years should be made out of the particular materials named. So, if you want to uphold the custom – flowers and boxes of chocolates notwith-standing – the list below gives the names generally associated with each year. They do vary slightly, however; paper is sometimes given for the first year, leather for the twelfth, ivory for the thirtieth, wool for the fortieth, and silk for the forty-fifth.

Anniversary	*Wedding*
First	Cotton
Second	Paper
Third	Leather
Fourth	Books
Fifth	Wood
Sixth	Sugar
Seventh	Wool
Eighth	Bronze
Ninth	Pottery
Tenth	Tin

Twelfth	Silk and Fine Linen
Fifteenth	Crystal
Twentieth	China
Twenty-fifth	Silver
Thirtieth	Pearl
Thirty-fifth	Coral
Fortieth	Ruby
Forty-fifth	Sapphire
Fiftieth	Golden
Fifty-fifth	Emerald
Sixtieth or Seventy-fifth	Diamond

PERSONAL WEDDING CHECKLISTS

CHECKLIST CONTENTS

1   The Engagement   96
2   The Register Office   97
3   The Church   99
4   Scotland   101
5   The Bride   102
6   The Bridegroom   105
7   The Bride's Mother   107
8   The Bride's Father   110
9   The Best Man   112
10 The Chief Bridesmaid   115
11 The Ushers   117
12 The Bridesmaids and Pages   118
13 Places During the Ceremony   119
14 The Procession to the Vestry   120
15 The Photographs   121
16 Seating Places at the Reception   123
17 At the Reception   124
18 Suggested Wedding List   125

PERSONAL CHECKLISTS

G ETTING ENGAGED and planning a wedding are very important times in anyone's life, so it is essential to make sure that as little as possible can go wrong or be forgotten.

Because there is so much to think about, so many people to see, plans to make and things to remember, these checklists were designed to simplify the problems and help you make sure that nothing is left out. By using the lists as an aid to your planning, you can remove some of the worries.

The checklists are simple to use. Just read them through and cross out any sections which do not apply to you. Then tick the relevant box when you have completed a job. You will then be able to see at a glance what you still have to do.

There are spaces for filling in dates, times or names, and you can write the names, addresses and telephone numbers of suppliers on the checklists for easy reference and last-minute checking. You may also wish to make a note of prices – if the parents of the bride have a second daughter, they may find this useful for her wedding.

To help relieve some of the organisation, different lists can be dealt with by different people. Checklist 10, for example, is designed to help the chief bridesmaid.

CHECKLIST 1: THE ENGAGEMENT

Announce decision to her parents ☑

Announce decision to his parents ☑

Arrange for parents to meet ☑

Make a list of those to be informed ☐

Tell relatives ☑

Tell close friends ☑

Engagement party/celebration ☐

Press announcement ☐
  A simple form may read:
  "The engagement is announced between James, son of
  Mr & Mrs A. Rogers of 14 Carlton Road, Wildhouse,
  Essex and Mary, daughter of Mr & Mrs D. Lock of 72
  Bridge Street, Rotown, Hampshire."

Buy the ring ☑

  Traditional ring ☐

  Family ring or heirloom ☐

  Antique ring ☐

  Birth-stone ☐

Present from her to him ☑
  Although not necessary, a ring, lighter, cuff-links
  or similar gift is acceptable.

CHECKLIST 2: THE REGISTER OFFICE

Both parties must be over 16 ☐

If under 18, obtain parents' consent ☐

For divorced persons, obtain a decree absolute ☐

Provide details of names, ages, addresses etc. ☐

Provide statements that there are no legal reasons why
the marriage should not take place ☐

Choose register office ☐

Obtain Superintendent Registrar's Certificate ☐

If both living in district for preceding
7 days, one partner can apply in person ☐

If living in different districts for
preceding 7 days, each partner must
apply in person to respective
Superintendent Registrars ☐

Notice entered in Superintendent
Registrar's notice book ☐

Obtain certificate (after 21 days) ☐

OR Obtain Superintendent Registrar's Certificate
and Licence ☐

If one partner living in district for
preceding 15 days, he/she can apply in
person ☐

Other partner living in England or Wales
at time notice given ☐

Notice entered in Superintendent
Registrar's notice book □

Obtain certificate (after one clear day) □

OR Obtain Registrar General's Licence □

Apply in person to Superintendent
Registrar □

Obtain licence □

Finalise date of ceremony .... □

Finalise place of ceremony .... □

CHECKLIST 3: THE CHURCH

Both parties must be over 16 ☑

If under 18, obtain parents' consent ☐

For divorced persons, obtain a decree absolute and agreement of the minister ☐

Choose church ☐

Apply to minister of church ☑

Arrange for publication of banns ☐

    Ask minister of church to publish banns ☐

    If one partner living in different parish, also arrange for banns to be called in that parish ☐

    If both partners living in different parishes, also arrange for banns to be called in those parishes ☐

    Banns to be read out during morning service on:

    1. .... ☐

    2. .... ☐

    3. .... ☐

    Attend calling of banns ☐

OR Obtain a common licence ☐

    If one partner living in parish for preceding 15 days, he/she can apply in person ☐

    Obtain licence ☐

OR Obtain a special licence ☐

   Apply to Archbishop of Canterbury ☐

   Provide sworn statement of reasons special
   licence required ☐

   Obtain licence ☐

OR Obtain Superintendent Registrar's Certificate ☐

   If one partner living in district for
   preceding 7 days, he/she can apply in
   person ☐

   Notice entered ☐

   Obtain certificate (after 21 days) ☐

Finalise date of ceremony .... ☑

Finalise place of ceremony .... ☑

CHECKLIST 4: SCOTLAND

Obtain marriage notice forms ☐

Return marriage notice forms with birth certificates, and death certificate or divorce decree certificate if second marriage ☐

Collect marriage schedule ☐

Finalise date of ceremony .... ☑

Finalise place of ceremony .... ☑

Sign marriage schedule and arrange for it to be signed by 2 witnesses and person who conducted the wedding ☐

Return marriage schedule to registrar ☐

CHECKLIST 5: THE BRIDE

Preparations (*with the bridegroom; ** with the bride's mother)

Discuss with minister*: ☑

   Church decorations ☐

   Music ☐

   Organist ☑

   Choir ☐

   Bells ☐

   Order of service ☑

   Fees ☑

   Confetti ☐

   Photographs in church ☐

Choose chief bridesmaid/matron of honour ☑

Choose bridesmaids ☑

Choose pages ☐

Draw up guest list** ☑

Arrange for wedding dress and attachments ☐

   Buy ☑

   Make ☑

   Hire ☐

Arrange for outfits for bridesmaids and pages ☐

    Buy ☑

    Make ☑

    Hire ☐

Book hairdressing appointment ☐

Order wedding cake and arrange for delivery** ✓

Order bouquets for self and bridesmaids and arrange for delivery** ☐

Order sprays for bride's and groom's mothers, and buttonholes for bridegroom, bride's and groom's fathers, best man and ushers, and arrange for delivery** ☐

Select and book photographer** ☐

Order wedding cars for wedding party to church and to reception** ☐

Write wedding present list ☐

Choose wedding breakfast menu** ☐

Choose wines** ☐

Arrange press announcement ☐

Choose going-away outfit and luggage ☑

Write thank-you letters for presents as they arrive ☐

Pack for honeymoon ☐

On the day

Give gifts to bridesmaids ☐

Take luggage and going-away outfit to reception ☐

At the church

Arrive last on father's right arm and proceed up the aisle followed by bridesmaids ☐

At chancel steps give bouquet and gloves to chief bridesmaid ☐

Allow chief bridesmaid to lift veil ☐

After service, with bridegroom follow minister to sign register ☐

Leave church with bridegroom ☐

After photographs, leave first with bridegroom for reception ☐

At the reception

Greet guests with bridegroom after parents ☐

With groom, cut cake ☐

After reception, change into going-away outfit ☐

Save flower from bouquet, and toss bouquet on leaving ☐

CHECKLIST 6: THE BRIDEGROOM

Preparations (*with bride)

Arrange for registrar or clergy* ☑

Choose best man ☑

Choose ushers ☐

Buy wedding ring* ☐

Arrange and pay for wedding outfit ☐

    Buy ☐

    Hire ☑

Plan, book and pay for honeymoon ☐

Organise and pay for stag party ☐

Arrange and pay for car from reception ☐

Buy bridesmaid's gifts ☐

Buy best man's gift ☐

Write speech for reception ☐

Pay for:

    Flowers of bride and attendants ☐

    Buttonholes and sprays ☐

    Car for self and best man to church ☐

    Car for bride and self to reception ☐

Choose going-away outfit and luggage ☑

Pack for honeymoon ☐

On the day

Give gift to best man ☐

Give money to best man for church fees ☐

Take luggage and going-away outfit to reception ☐

Take going-away car to reception ☐

At the church

Arrive with best man at .... ☐

Step up to altar when bride arrives ☐

After service, with bride follow minister to sign
   register ☐

Leave church with bride ☐

After photographs, leave first with bride for reception ☐

At the reception

Greet guests with bride after parents ☐

Respond to toast "The bride and groom", give
   speech and propose toast to "The Bridesmaids" ☐

With bride, cut cake ☐

After reception, change into going-away outfit ☐

Collect documents etc. from best man ☐

CHECKLIST 7: THE BRIDE'S MOTHER

Preparations (** with bride)

Draw up guest list** ☐

Arrange printing of invitations ☑

Arrange printing of order of service cards ☑

Send invitations ☐

List acceptances received ☐

Draw up final guest list ☐

Prepare seating plan ☐

Arrange wedding outfit ☑

    Buy ☐

    Make ☐

Order bouquets for bride and bridesmaids and
    arrange for delivery** ☑

Order sprays for self and groom's mother, and
    buttonholes for bridegroom, bride's and
    groom's fathers, best man and ushers,
    and arrange for delivery** ☐

Arrange church decorations ☐

Select and book photographer** ☐

Make arrangements for reception at .... ☐

    Home ☐

Hotel ☑

Restaurant ☐

Private hall ☐

Make catering arrangements ☐

Self ☐

Professional caterers ☐

Choose wedding breakfast menu** ☐

Choose wines** ☐

Arrange for table decorations ☐

Arrange accommodation for guests ☐

Arrange for printed napkins ☐

Arrange for printed place setting cards ☑

Arrange for musicians/entertainment ☑

Order wedding cars for wedding party to church and
to reception** ☐

Order wedding cake and arrange for delivery** ☑

Buy wedding cake boxes ☐

Arrange for neighbour to lock house after bride
and father have left ☐

At the church

Arrive before the bride at .... ☐

After service, with groom's father follow bride's father and groom's mother to sign register ☐

Leave church with groom's father ☐

After photographs, leave for reception with parents after bridesmaids and best man ☐

At the reception

With bride's father, greet guests ☐

When all guests have arrived, give signal for wedding breakfast to begin ☐

Arrange display of gifts ☐

Arrange changing room for bride ☐

Arrange display of proof photographs ☐

Take photograph orders from family and guests ☐

After the wedding

Send pieces of cake to relatives/friends who could not attend wedding ☑

Give order to photographer ☐

Collect and distribute photographs ☐

CHECKLIST 8: THE BRIDE'S FATHER

Preparations

Arrange for wedding outfit ☐

    Buy ☐

    Hire ☐

Write speech for reception ☐

Pay for:
    Reception ☐

    Flowers to decorate church and reception ☐

    Wedding dress and bridesmaids' dresses ☐

    Wedding cake ☐

    Photographer ☐

    Wedding cars ☐

    Press announcement ☐

    Hairdressing ☐

    Invitations and order of service printing ☐

Keep buttonhole at home when other sprays/
buttonholes taken to church ☐

At the church

Arrive last with bride on right arm and proceed up
aisle ☐

At appropriate moment, give bride's right hand to
minister ☐

After service, with groom's mother follow best
man and chief bridesmaid to sign register ☐

Leave church with groom's mother ☐

After photographs, leave for reception with parents
after bridesmaids and best man ☐

At the reception

With bride's mother greet guests ☐

When called by best man, give speech and
propose toast to bride and groom ☐

CHECKLIST 9: THE BEST MAN

Preparations

Arrange and pay for own outfit ☐

    Buy ☐

    Hire ☐

Check that groom and ushers have organised outfits ☐

Write speech for reception ☐

Help to organise stag party ☐

Check parking facilities at church and reception ☐

Check groom has all necessary documents for wedding and honeymoon ☐

Arrange for car to take groom and self to church ☐

On the day

Check that bridegroom's luggage is ready ☐

Check that bridegroom's change of clothes is ready ☐

Arrange for going-away car to be parked at reception and keep keys ☐

Have tickets and documents for honeymoon ☐

Have cash for church fees ☐

Keep wedding rings safe ☐

Have documents for wedding ☐

Collect buttonholes from bride's mother and
  take to church ☐

Collect telegrams and order of service sheets from
  bride's mother ☐

Collect bridegroom at .... o'clock and take to
  church ☐

At the church

Ensure that ushers know duties ☐

Hand order of service sheets to ushers ☐

Make sure bridegroom, groom's father, self and
  ushers have buttonholes, and bride's and
  groom's mothers have sprays ☐

Pay fees to minister ☐

Wait on right of groom and hand over ring at
  appropriate time ☐

After service with chief bridesmaid follow bride
  and groom to sign register ☐

Leave church with chief bridesmaid ☐

Usher couple to places for photographs ☐

Make sure ushers have arranged transport for
  guests to reception ☐

After photographs, see couple to car to take them to
  reception ☐

Leave for reception with bridesmaids after bride
  and groom ☐

At the reception

Offer drinks to guests ☐

Take charge of any late wedding presents ☐

Place luggage in car for honeymoon ☐

Call on speakers ☐

Respond to toast of "The bridesmaids", give speech
and read telegrams ☐

Hand over documents, keys etc. for honeymoon ☐

See couple to car after reception ☐

After the wedding

Return wedding outfits of groom and self if hired ☐

CHECKLIST 10: THE CHIEF BRIDESMAID (MATRON OF HONOUR)

Preparations

Arrange for own outfit (pay for it unless unsuitable for wear at other times) ☐

On the day

Help to dress the bride for the ceremony ☐

Make sure bouquets are ready for bride and bridesmaids ☐

Look after bridesmaids and pages ☐

At the church

Assemble with bridesmaids and pages in church porch ☐

Arrange bride's dress, veil and train for procession up the aisle ☐

Take bride's bouquet and gloves at chancel steps ☐

Lift bride's veil ☐

After service, with best man follow bride and groom to sign register ☐

Return bouquet and gloves to bride in vestry ☐

Leave church with best man after bride and groom ☐

After photographs, leave for reception with best man and other bridesmaids, after bride and groom ☐

At the reception

Offer drinks to guests ☐

Check that bride's going-away outfit is ready ☐

Check that bride's luggage is ready ☐

Help bride change into going-away clothes ☐

See bride to car ☐

After the wedding

Return bride's and own outfit if hired ☐

CHECKLIST 11: THE USHERS

Preparations

Arrange and pay for own outfits ☐

   Buy ☐

   Hire ☐

At the church

Arrive at the church at .... ☐

Collect order of service sheets from best man ☐

Conduct guests to their pews and hand out order
   of service sheets ☐

Ensure guests have transport to reception ☐

At the reception

Offer drinks to guests ☐

After the wedding

Return outfit if hired ☐

CHECKLIST 12: THE BRIDESMAIDS AND PAGES

Preparations

Bride will arrange for outfits ☑

At the church

Arrive at the church porch at .... ☐

Follow the chief bridesmaid up the aisle ☐

Wait at chancel steps/sit down as instructed ☐

After signing of register, follow chief bridesmaid
and best man out of church ☐

After photographs, leave for reception with chief
brides-maid and best man, after the bride and
groom ☐

At the reception

Offer drinks to guests (older attendants only) ☐

Carry cake to guests ☐

CHECKLIST 13: PLACES DURING THE CEREMONY

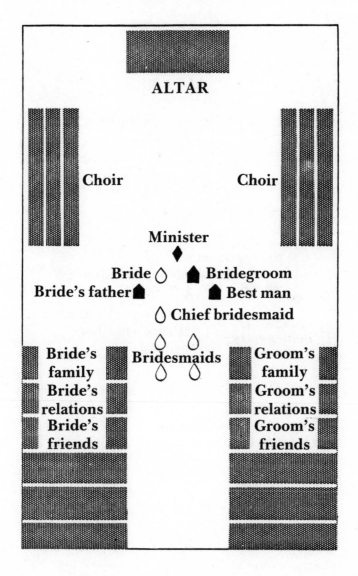

CHECKLIST 14: THE PROCESSION TO THE VESTRY

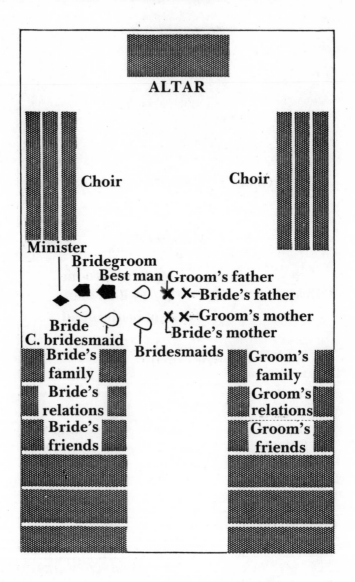

CHECKLIST 15: THE PHOTOGRAPHS

Select and book photographer ☐

Photographs may be requested of: ☐

   Bride's dressing table ☐

   Before leaving for the wedding ☐

   Leaving the house ☐

   The best man and groom before the ceremony ☐

   Arriving at the church/register office ☐

   Inside the church (with minister's permission) ☐

   Signing the register (with minister's permission) ☐

   Leaving the church/register office ☐

   Bride and groom ☐

   Couple with parents ☐

   Couple with best man and bridesmaids ☐

   Couple with bride's family ☐

   Couple with groom's family ☐

   Couple with friends ☐

   Bridesmaids and attendants ☐

   At the reception ☐

   Cutting the cake ☐

Discuss any special effects required, e.g. couple in wine glass ☐

Arrange for proof photographs to be made available at the reception ☐

Take orders for photographs from family and guests ☐

Give order to photographer ☐

Distribute photographs ☐

CHECKLIST 16: SEATING PLACES AT THE RECEPTION

Arrange seating plan ☐

TOP TABLE

1 Groom's mother	6 Groom's father
2 Bride's father	7 Chief bridesmaid
3 Bride	8 Best man
4 Bridegroom	9 Groom's family
5 Bride's mother	10 Bride's family

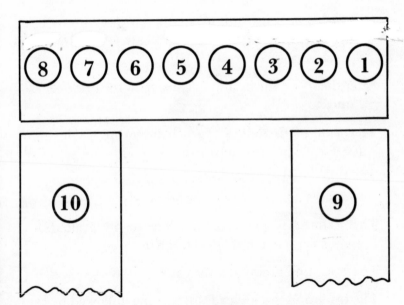

Variations on the seating may be made although the top table is usually reserved for the wedding party. Alternating the sexes is usual. The families can be mixed.

CHECKLIST 17: AT THE RECEPTION

As guests arrive they should be greeted by:
   The bride's father and mother ☐

   The groom's father and mother ☐

   The bride and groom ☐

Attendants and ushers should offer drinks and chat pleasantly ☐

When all the guests have arrived, the hostess (the bride's mother) should give the signal for the wedding breakfast to begin ☐

If champagne is used for toasts only, it should be left until after the meal and served just before the speeches begin ☐

After the meal, the best man calls upon the bride's father to speak ☐

The bride's father gives a speech and proposes the toast to "The bride and groom" ☐

The bridegroom responds, gives a speech and proposes a toast to "The bridesmaids" ☐

The best man responds on behalf of the bridesmaids, gives a speech and reads out the telegrams ☐

The bride and groom cut the cake ☐

The bride and groom lead the dancing, followed by the best man and the chief bridesmaid, and the parents of the bride and groom ☐

CHECKLIST 18: SUGGESTED WEDDING LIST

Many of these ideas can be divided into several specific suggestions, for example, glasses can be dived into the various types you would like. You may wish to specify particular colours or styles you would prefer for many items. You will also need to consider the more personal gifts you would like to add.

Apron
Baking tins
Bathroom cabinet
Blankets
Bread bin
Bookcase
Bowl, bucket etc.
Carpets
Carpet sweeper
Casserole dishes
Corkscrew
Coffee grinder
Coffee percolator
Coffee table
Cookery book
Cruet set
Cushions
Cutlery
Dinner service
Door mat
Duvet
Egg rack
Electric drill

Feather duster
Food processor
Fridge
Garden fork
Garden furniture
Garden spade
Glasses
Hoover
Kitchen knives
Laundry basket
Lawn mower
Mirror
Mincer
Mixer
Oven
Oven gloves
Pedal bin
Personal stationery
Pictures
Pillows
Place mats
Pyrex dishes
Rugs

Saucepans
Saw, hammer etc.
Scales
Sheets
Spice rack
Storage jars
Table and chairs
Table lamp
Tablecloth
Tea service
Tea towels
Telephone table
Three-piece suite
Trolley
Toaster
Tool box
Tools
Towels
Vases
Vegetable rack
Wall can opener
Washing machine
Wine rack

INDEX

abroad 25
age 19
anniversaries 91–2
announcement, engagement 10–11, 26
  wedding 39
appearance, bride's 42
assurance, companies 80
  life 84
attendants 33–4

bank 77, 80, 81, 82, 83
  account 77
  loan 77
  manager 77
  mortgages 81–2
banns 13, 14–15, 24, 58
bells 26
best man 33–4, 36, 43, 45, 46, 47, 48, 55, 56–8, 59, 60, 66
  checklist 112–14
birth certificate 23, 25
birth-stones 11–12
bouquets 37, 38, 40, 44, 46, 55, 59
breakfast, wedding 53
bride 8, 29, 31, 33, 34, 37, 42, 43, 44, 46, 47, 48, 49, 50, 51, 53, 54, 55, 57, 58, 59, 65, 66, 67, 68, 72, 86, 88, 89, 90
  checklist 102–4
  father 36, 39, 40, 43, 46, 48, 54, 65, 69 see also parents, bride's
  father's checklist 110–11
  mother 37, 46, 48, 54, 57, 58, 69 see also parents, bride's
  mother's checklist 107–8

bridegroom 8, 31, 33, 34, 35, 36, 40–1, 43, 46, 47, 48, 49, 50, 51, 53, 54, 55, 56, 57, 58, 59, 61, 65, 66, 67, 68, 72, 90
  checklist 105–6
  father 36, 48, 54 see also parents, bridegroom's
  mother 37, 48, 54 see also parents, bridegroom's
bridesmaids 34, 46, 48, 55, 57, 59, 66
  checklist 118
  chief 34, 43, 46, 47, 48, 59–60
  chief bridesmaid's checklist 115–16
building societies 77, 80, 81, 82, 83, 85
buttonholes 37, 58

cake 55
  boxes 30, 55
  cutting 54, 55
cars 40, 57
catering 53
ceremony 27, 45–52, 68, 72
choir 26, 46
church, checklist 99–100
  decorations 37–8
  of England 13–16, 45, 49
  fees 26
confetti 48
credit cards 78

dancing 55
dates, lucky 88–9
death certificate 23

denominations, other than C of
  E 20–1
District Registrar of Marriages 24
divorce 19, 27, 29, 67, 68
  decree 23
documents, foreign 23, 25
dresses, bride's 35, 40, 59, 68, 86–7,
  90
  bridesmaids' 35, 40
drinks 53

engagement 8–12
  announcement 10–11, 26
  breaking off 12
  celebration 12
  checklist 96
  list 10, 28
  presents 12

families 10
  bride's 57
  bridegroom's 57
fees 39–41, 58
finance 9, 74–8, 79
  houses 82
financial outgoings 76, 77, 78, 79
flowers 37–8, 40
  church 37–8, 40
  reception 37–8, 40
  register office 38
friends 9, 48, 67
  bride's 57
  bridegroom's 57
friendship 8

going away clothes 43, 55, 58, 60
guest list 28

hair 42
home, setting up 74, 75
honeymoon 41, 55, 57, 68, 72–3, 90
  documents 58, 73
  luggage 58
house, buying 75, 79–85
  renting 75, 76, 79

in laws 10
insurance 75
  companies 80, 82
invitations 27–30, 40, 67

Jewish ceremonies 19, 50–2

legal regulations 19–20, 22–3, 25
  costs 40
licence 24
  common 13, 15
  ordinary 15
  Registrar General's 17, 18, 19
  special 13, 14, 16, 19, 24
loans 77, 78, 79, 81, 83
  bridging 82 see also mortgage
local authorities 80, 81, 82

make-up 42, 43
marriage notice form 22, 23
  preparation course 26
  schedule 23
  (Scotland) Act 1977 22
matron of honour 34 see also
  bridesmaid, chief
menus 53
ministers 14, 15, 16, 21, 22, 26, 27,
  37, 45, 46, 47, 58, 71
mortgage 77, 79, 80, 81, 82–3, 84,
  85
  brokers 80, 82
  endowment 83–4
  option 83
  repayment 83
music 26, 46, 60

name, changing 70–1
National House Building Council
  84, 85
newspaper 10, 39, 40
Northern Ireland 24

Order of Service sheets 30, 57, 58

pages checklist 118

parental consent 19
parents 10, 39, 59
  bride's 28, 29, 33, 55, 58, 66, 67, 69 *see also* bride's father, bride's mother
  bridegroom's 57, 69 *see also* bridegroom's father, bridegroom's mother
parking facilities 53, 56
passports 58, 71, 73
photographs 27, 36, 38–9, 40, 42, 43, 47, 48
  checklist 121–2
postponement 30
presents 30–3, 58
  best man's 34, 40
  bride's mother and father's 41, 43
  bridesmaids' 34, 40, 43
  checklist 125
  displaying 33
  list 31–2, 75
  ushers' 40

Quaker ceremonies 19, 48–9

receiving line 43, 54, 69
reception 33, 40, 48, 53–5, 57, 58, 60, 61, 66, 68, 72
  checklist 124
register office 16, 18, 21, 24, 27, 35, 38
  office checklist 97–8
  signing of 43, 46, 47, 59–60
  signing, procession checklist 120
registrar 16, 17, 21, 22, 23, 26, 50, 71
  assistant 22
  certificate 24
rehearsal 45
relations, prohibited 20
relationships 9

relatives 10, 48, 67
replies 30
rings 49, 50, 51
  engagement 11, 40
  wedding 11, 40, 46, 47, 57, 58, 90
Roman Catholic weddings 49–50
Royal Navy 21

saving 77, 80, 81
Scotland 22–4
  checklist 101
seating in church 45, 69
  church checklist 119
  at reception 46, 69
  reception checklist 123
second marriage 67–9
service of blessing 27
social security benefits 75
solicitors 82
speeches 43, 54, 55, 57, 61–6, 68, 69
stag party 40, 41, 57
suits 58
  morning 36
Superintendent Registrar 17, 18, 24, 27, 48, 49
  certificate 16, 17
  certificate and licence 17, 18
superstitions 86–90
surveys 85

tax 74–5, 80, 82, 83
telegrams 55, 58, 66
thank-you letters 30, 31, 32–3
toasts 43, 53, 54, 55, 57, 61–6, 68, 69

ushers 34, 36, 57
  checklist 117

video 39

witnesses 19, 22, 23, 49